Winning at PRICING
How High-Tech Product Managers
Can Avoid Common Mistakes
That Defeat Pricing Strategies

By Dawn Pugh

Kaleah Publishing

KALEAH

For information, consulting, live events, speaker bookings— or interviews for radio, TV, print, or online sources—and other services, please email kaleahpublishing@gmail.com.

THE FREE PRESS

A Division of Simon & Shuster Inc.
1230 Avenue of the Americas
New York, NY 10020

Library of Congress Cataloging-in-Publication Data

Porter, Michael E.

Competitive advantage: creating and sustaining superior performance: with a new introduction/Michael E. Porter

p. cm.

Originally published: New York: Free Press;
London Collier Macmillan, c1985

Includes bibliographical references and index.

1. Competition.   2. Industrial management   I. Title.

HD41.P668   1998

658–dc21   98–9581

ISBN 0-684-84146-0

This book is dedicated, in loving memory, to Abby.

Table of Contents

Preface

After spending the majority of my marketing career focused on pricing, competitive pricing, and competitive analysis, I have written this book for high-tech product managers on how to win at pricing. High-tech refers to product managers in the information technology and telecommunications industries.

The book is dedicated to best practices to avoid common mistakes that defeat pricing strategies. The main goal is to help high-tech product managers create value that aligns with a premium price. Throughout this book "product" implies a physical product or a service as a product.

When a product manager develops the marketing strategy for a product he or she conducts market, segmentation, targeting, and positioning analysis. The overall goal is to create the positioning of the product for the markets he or she intends to target. This positioning should communicate the value of a product by demonstrating the advantages it creates for the buyer.

Establishing value in product positioning is not as easy as one might think. I have witnessed many failures by product managers in articulating value in the positioning of a product. When a product manager fails in the positioning, he or she will have a hard time winning at pricing since the positioning is what attracts a buyer to pay a premium price.

> "A firm creates value for a buyer that justifies a premium price (or preference at an equal price) through two mechanisms: by lowering buyer cost or by raising buyer performance,"[1] writes Michael Porter, in his book *Competitive Advantage – Creating and Sustaining Superior Performance*; however, Mr. Porter points out, "Buyers will not pay for value that they do not perceive, no matter how real it may be. Thus, the price premium a firm commands will reflect both the value actually delivered to its buyer and the extent to which the buyer perceives this value. A firm that delivers only modest value, but signals it more effectively may actually command a higher price than a firm that delivers higher value but signals it poorly. In the long run, the upper limit of the price premium a firm can command reflects its actual impact on buyer value—impact on buyer cost and performance relative to competitors. Through effective signaling of value, a firm may be able to command a price in excess of true value for a time. Eventually, however, the failure of a firm to deliver perceived value to match its price tends to become known, partly through the efforts of competitors. The converse is less true, however. By failing to signal its value effectively, a firm may never realize the price premium its actual value deserves. [2]

To summarize Michael Porter's thoughts, if the product satisfies one or both of the two mechanisms, then express the value in the positioning of the product. On the other hand, if the buyer does not perceive the actual value delivered, the positioning does not reflect the value of the product. Hence, effectively positioning the value is instrumental to the success of a product.

Likewise, before a product manager can launch a product she or he must create the packaging strategy. The attractiveness of the packaging strategy is also instrumental to the success of a product. For high-tech product managers, this requires reducing complexity, creating attractiveness, and providing clarity in the packaging strategy.

The creativity of the product manager is what will make the product attractive. Unfortunately, too often creativity is overlooked in developing the packaging strategy. The product manager's focus on the appeal of the technology overshadows any focus on the attractiveness of the packaging. When a product manager overlooks making the packaging attractive, they will have a hard time winning at pricing since the attractiveness is what makes the product ideal for a buyer to pay a premium price.

For these reasons, I realized the advice I give in this book. I did not learn it in graduate school. It came from over a decade of experiences in pricing products, analyzing competitor pricing, developing business metrics, and being engaged in pricing policies and processes. What's more, because I kept seeing the same mistakes repeatedly occur, it became a call to action for me. I want to help product managers win at pricing. This is why I wrote the book. To teach high-tech product managers how to avoid the common mistakes that defeat pricing strategies.

To every product manager that reads this book, my goal is for you to walk away understanding these three principles:

1. How to make value obvious for your product.
2. How to make your product attractive.
3. How to keep the value and attractiveness of your product.

We have all heard the old saying, "price is in the eye of the customer," so if you understand how to accomplish these three principles there is no reason why you should not be winning at pricing.

This book would not have been possible without the gracious support from Michael Porter, the Bishop William Lawrence University Professor at Harvard Business School, for allowing me to use excerpts from his book *Competitive Advantage Creating and Sustaining Superior Performance*. Dr. Porter wrote his book in 1985 when the high-tech industry was in its infancy; however, as the reader will see throughout this book, his principles on modern strategy are as relevant today as they were at the time of his writing. I have always been fascinated by his work, and it has guided me in my career to hold on to the truths he revealed. I am deeply honored to be able to reference his work in *Winning at Pricing, How High-Tech Product Managers Can Avoid Common Mistakes That Defeat Pricing Strategies*.

I would also like to thank Joe Francesconi for giving me my wings; and Gary Lau, Dennis Wolfe, Simon Williams, Sandy Orlando, Truls Myklebust, and Mike Schmidt for putting me in situations that inspired me to write this book. While I was not able to accomplish everything I wanted in some of the situations, each experience built on the others, allowing me to understand the common mistakes that defeat pricing strategies for product managers in the high-tech industry.

Lastly, I would like to thank Pat Power for the design of the book cover, interior book design, and copy-edit contributions. Pat is a talented designer and a valuable resource. For example, the large barcode you see on the front cover is a typeface [font]. It's called CODE-3OF9X1. The keystrokes used spell WINNINGATPRICING. Pat's portfolio can be viewed at www.PatPowerDesign.com. I would also like to thank Lauren Johnson for the copy-edit; and Kate Power, my good friend and neighbor, for the author photo. Lauren is an exceptional copy editor and marketing communications expert. Her professionalism and charming personality made working with her an enjoyable experience. Lauren can be reach at ljwriter87@gmail.com.

Introduction

One can easily say that Apple is one of the most innovative companies in the world. Over the past three decades, they have released five core products that have changed the world: the Mac, the iPod, iTunes, the iPhone, and the iPad.

In fact, I will never forget the first time I experienced an Apple product. The year was 1989, and I was a sales systems engineer at Apple. For the two years I worked at the company, I can say it was a fantastic journey working in a culture surrounded by slogans like, "Think Different," and concepts like the "Knowledge Navigator." What is more, I was totally blown away by the products.

What is relevant about Apple to this book and was obvious back then as well as today, is that Apple has always sold its products at a premium price. So, why does Apple sell its products at a premium price, you might be wondering? The short answer is that Apple understands the value of the innovation they are creating. It is not a laptop, media player, online music store, phone, or tablet. The value Apple creates is the user experience and people are willing to pay a premium price for the experience they provide.

What's more, by effectively signaling value, Apple is able to achieve the price premium their products actual value deserves. For example, the slogan Steve Jobs used when Apple released the first iPhone was, "The internet in your pocket." A powerful statement in describing the iPhone that effectively signals value in the user experience. Hence, Apple priced the iPhone to the value established by the positioning, which was at a premium price; $499 (US) for the 4GB model and $599 (US) for the 8GB model.

Cisco is another company historically known for selling its products at a premium price; however, while Apple's sells what I call crossover consumer products that are sold to both consumers and businesses, Cisco predominately sells industrial products to businesses. As a result, the value Cisco creates is solving business problems and businesses are willing to pay a premium price for the products and solutions they offer. For example, the positioning for Cisco's switches is "Secure. Reliable. Seamless. Cisco switches scale to meet the needs of networks of all sizes." A dominant statement to describe its switches that effectively signals value in solving business problems.

This is a fundamental distinction to understand because a product manager must position the value of their product to match the expectation of the market he or she intends to target. Cisco would never position its switches as a user experience because businesses buy switches to solve a problem such as reliability and performance on their networks. Likewise, Apple would never position the iPhone as solving a problem because consumers buy smartphones for the user experience, such as touch screen calling, visual voice, a soft keyboard, camera, or large screen.

What is more, it is not defensible to say that a consumer bought an iPhone to solve a problem. Even if the reason for purchasing an iPhone was to satisfy his or her need to have email, text messaging, and web browsing on one phone, since there are less expensive smartphones in the market that offer the same applications on another smartphone. Therefore, if a consumer purchases an iPhone, it was purchased for the user experience or the prestige or status that comes from owning an iPhone.

I am not saying Apple could not position the iPhone as solving consumer problems or that Cisco could not position its switches as a user experience for businesses, but the positioning would be less effective at signaling the value of the iPhone and the switches to achieve the price premium. What's more, buyers would be confused since the price would not reflect the actual value perceived by the buyer. Thus, the better the positioning articulates the actual value of the product, the more reasonable the price will seem to the buyer.

Michael Porter on Buyer Value[3]

A firm creates value for a buyer that justifies a premium price (or preference at an equal price) through two mechanisms:

- by lowering buyer cost
- by raising buyer performance

For industrial, commercial, and institutional buyers, differentiation requires that a firm be uniquely able to *create competitive advantage for its buyer* in ways besides selling to them at a lower price. If a firm is able to lower its buyer's cost or enhance its buyer's performance, the buyer will be willing to pay a premium. If the components supplied by a well-respected bicycle parts supplier allow a bicycle assembler to improve differentiation and thereby charge a higher price, for example, the assembler will be willing to pay a premium for the components. Similarly, the fact that Kodak's Ektaprint copier lowers the cost of a finished set of collated documents with a recirculating document feeder and an in-line automatic stapler, which reduces the buyer's personnel cost means that the buyer is willing to pay a premium for the copier. In both instances, the firm was able to enhance the competitive advantage of its buyer even though not selling its product at a cheaper price. The principle is the same for households and individual consumers, though the measurement of buyer cost and particularly buyer performance may be more subtle. For household buyers, the cost of a product includes not only financial costs but also time or convenience costs. The cost of time for a consumer reflects the opportunity cost of using it elsewhere, as well as the implicit cost of frustration, annoyance, or exertion. Buyer value results from lowering any of these costs for the buyer. A refrigerator that uses less electricity than other refrigerators can command a premium price. A vacuum cleaner that saves vacuuming time and reduces exertion is also valuable to the household buyer. Offering direct marketing that saves the buyer shopping time may not be valuable if the buyer enjoys shopping, however.

Raising buyer performance for consumers involves raising their level of satisfaction or meeting their needs. If a TV set's better picture quality and faster warm up time lead to more satisfaction in watching it relative to competitors' sets, for example, the buyer will be willing to pay a premium. Status or prestige are important needs just as are the features of a product or its quality. Although it may be difficult to value buyer performance for consumers, their value chains will suggest the important dimensions of satisfaction.

Industrial, commercial, and institutional buyers sometimes resemble consumers in instances where their objectives are not solely profits or revenue growth. Buyers may value a supplier that provides satisfaction or prestige for executives or other employees even if it does not contribute to the profit of the company. This reflects the differences that often exist between employees and company goals. Similarly, a hospital values a diagnostic device that yields better treatment even if the hospital does not earn higher profit as a result. This reflects both the goal of providing quality patient care and the fact that a large number of hospitals are nonprofit institutions. Many organizations have other goals in addition to profitability even if they are profit making, which may enter into buyer value.

Winning at Pricing is about creating value for products through best practices I have learned over the past 15 years of my career. In this book, product managers will learn how to avoid common mistakes that can defeat pricing strategies. In the first chapter, I will share how to build models to determine if the price of a product is right. The second chapter explores how to uncover the value of a product and how to make the value obvious in the positioning. In the third chapter, I reveal strategies on how to make the packaging of a product attractive. The fourth chapter focuses on establishing pricing policies to protect the value of a product. Lastly, in chapter five I will reveal the implications of "price is in the eye of the customer." So, let's get started.

1 The Price Isn't Right

I begin this book explaining how to conduct a pricing strategy analysis and review a pricing strategy. This is something every product manager should do on a regular basis. The reason is simple. Since the global economic downturn in 2008, the forces at work in every industry have changed. Businesses have been under pressure because of reduced investment by their customers. Let's be honest, no company went unscathed. Every business had to reduce spending, reprioritize projects, and create new business models to survive the economic downturn. As a result, product managers must examine the pricing strategy of their product as it applies to their customers' present situation.

The global economic downturn in 2008 affected every product in the high-tech industry. Some products survived while others did not. Even now, almost five years later, the products that survived are not completely out of the woods. It may not be that the product isn't viable for the company. It may be that the price is not right.

For example, a product manager for a network equipment company manages a product line of four data center switches that scale from the 5 slots to 20 slots. The product line has been priced using a product line pricing strategy to reflect the benefits of the increase in switching capacity across the range. Nonetheless, because of the economic downturn, customers are more reluctant to pay a premium price; therefore, an alternative pricing strategy the product manager could consider is to add a razor and blade pricing strategy on top of the product line pricing strategy. Specifically, a razor and blade pricing strategy involves charging a lower entry price for the base configuration of the data center switches and recovering the margin and more from the sale of additional I/O modules. This way the product manager is responding to his or her customers' present situation of having to reduce spending, while ensuring the ability to recapture the margin in the future.

The razor and blade pricing strategy is just one of many ways for a product manager to price a product or product line. The key is finding the right one. This can be accomplished by conducting a pricing strategy analysis.

How to Conduct a Pricing Strategy Analysis

In this section, I will walk through the three-step approach I use to conduct a pricing strategy analysis. The three steps are as follows:

- Product and Gross Margin Analysis
- Real World Cost of Ownership Analysis
- Packaging Analysis

Conducting the Product and Gross Margin Analysis

The product and gross margin analysis will give the product manager a clear picture of their current pricing strategy. It can easily be done on one spreadsheet in excel. To conduct the analysis requires both the BOM (bill of materials) and COGS (cost of goods sold) for the product, which can be obtained from the operations and finance departments.

When requesting the BOM from operations, be sure to ask for a component breakdown of the BOM. It is required to conduct a packaging analysis. Note that the COGS obtained from the finance department will be a higher cost than the BOM since COGS include the BOM and the operational costs associated with the product, such as labor and allocated overhead.

To create the model for the product and gross margin analysis add the following columns at the top of the excel spreadsheet and fill in the product's information or ask the I.T. department to create the spreadsheet from the company's business intelligence system, e.g., Business Objects. Then, highlight the header of the columns in the color of your choice.

1. Product Family
2. Product Name
3. List Price
4. BOM (Bill of Materials)
5. COGS (Cost of Goods Sold) The equation should equal BOM+ burden cost
6. Product Margin – The equation should equal 1–(COGS/List Price)
7. Average Discount – Ask the finance department or use the highest channel partner discount.
8. Gross Margin = 1–(COGS/(List Price *(1–Average Discount)))
9. NET Price = List Price * (1–Average Discount)

Once the spreadsheet is set up, take a close look at both the product and gross margins. Are the gross margins in the range of what is healthy for a product in the industry that it competes? Note the range for healthy gross margins is unique to every industry. For example, healthy gross margins in the telecom equipment market are in the 62% – 67% range; therefore, if the product's average discount is 42%, product margins must be above 78% to achieve healthy gross margins in the 62% – 67% range. On the other hand, healthy gross margins in the application software industry range from 72% – 80%; therefore, if the product's average discount is 42%, product margins must be above 84% to achieve gross margins in the 72% – 80% range.

For that reason, if the product manager does not know the industry range for their product's gross margins, she or he should ask the finance department or review the 10K of competitors. This is very important since low gross margins will reflect poorly on a company's earning. Specifically, low gross margins can negatively affect the stock price of a publicly traded company. It can also make it difficult for a startup company to attract venture capital. Most importantly, low gross margins are an indication of poor product performance, which raises many questions that the product manager must be prepared to respond to on a moment's notice.

Understanding the gross margins within the industry average will tell a product manager how their product is performing against the competition; however, if the gross margins are lower than the industry average, it is a clear indication that the product manager must take corrective action to improve them. Specifically, when gross margins are unhealthy, either the product margins are too low or the average discount is too high. Typically, low product margins indicate a rational for making the product price competitive. If this is the case, I highly recommend changing the pricing strategy. There are many other ways to make the product price competitive than to directly affect the product margins. On the other hand, higher average discounts indicate that the value of the product is not obvious, since customers are more reluctant to pay a premium price. In the next chapter, I will discuss product value in detail. However, unless the product manager is purposely using a penetration pricing strategy that sets the price artificially low in order to gain market share with the intent to increase the price once the goal is achieved, the product manager must do everything he or she can to achieve healthy gross margins. More to the point, if the product creates a strong competitive advantage for its buyers, the product manager should raise the product margins to reflect the competitive advantage.

Conducting the Real World Cost of Ownership Analysis

The second step of a pricing strategy analysis is to conduct a real-world cost of ownership analysis. The reason for doing the analysis is to determine if the product's differentiation is uniquely able to create competitive advantage for its buyers. For example, several years ago I conducted a cost of ownership analysis for a service provider edge-router. The request came a few weeks after I had completed a pricing analysis that determined the product had a price advantage over the competition. I cannot say with certainty that the outcome of the pricing analysis led to the request for the cost of ownership analysis, but it was the right thing to do.

Although the product had strong differentiation, the positioning of the product did not articulate that the product was uniquely able to create competitive advantage for its buyers. Therefore, instead of building the model to cover all the applications of the product, I created the model based on a case study using only one application of the product. My reason for doing it this way was to place the product in a real-world scenario and then compare it against the competition. Some might argue that a cost of ownership analysis should cover every application of the product. I disagree. Every time I have seen a product manager create an all-inclusive model, it became so complex that it concealed weaknesses the buyer could uncover. Regardless, when conducting a real-world cost of ownership analysis as part of a pricing strategy analysis, I recommend that the product manager use only one application of the product. This will make the differentiation of the product very clear in the model, but if the product manager feels he or she must cover every application, then a real-world cost of ownership analysis should be conducted for each application separately. The outcome of my real-world cost of ownership analysis demonstrated that the service provider edge-router had a significant competitive advantage in CAPEX and OPEX savings. Most importantly, the real-world cost of ownership analysis demonstrated that the product's differentiation was uniquely able to create competitive advantage for its buyers. Specifically, the outcome of the real-world cost of ownership analysis revealed that the service provider edge-router offered a higher port density per rack and lower annual recurring costs for rack, power, HVAC, and security—in the real world that translates into CAPEX and OPEX savings for service providers. As a result, the product manager was uniquely able to create competitive advantage for his prospects instead of selling to them at a lower price.

This is the reason for conducting a real-world cost of ownership analysis. The intent is to determine how a product's differentiation is uniquely able to create competitive advantage for its buyers. Typically, competitive advantages reduce costs, gain efficiency, maximize revenue, increase productivity, or reduce time to market.

Michael Porter on Lowering Buyer Costs and Raising Buyer Performance[4]

Lowering Buyer Costs. Anything a firm can do that lowers the buyer's total cost of using a product or other buyer costs represents a potential basis for differentiation. Actions that lower the cost of buyer value activities representing a significant fraction of the buyer's cost constitutes the most significant opportunities. There are frequently many ways to lower buyer cost if a firm has a sophisticated understanding of how buyers use its product and how its various marketing, delivery, and other activities affect buyer costs.

A firm can lower its buyer's cost in a number of ways:

- Lower delivery, installation, or financing cost
- Lower the required rate of usage of the product
- Lower the direct cost of using the product, such as labor, fuel, maintenance, required space
- Lower the indirect cost of using the product, or the impact of the product on other value activities. For example, a light component may reduce the transport costs of the end product
- Lower the buyer cost in other value activities unconnected with the physical product
- Lower the risk of product failure and thus the buyer's expected cost of failure.

Table 4–1 list some of the ways in which a firm's product itself can lower the buyer's direct cost of use. In addition to lowering buyer cost through its product characteristics as illustrated by the examples in Table 4–1, a firm can lower its buyer's cost of use through many other value activities. Reliability of deliveries reduces buyer inventory, and short lead times in supplying spare parts reduce downtime. Ordering and billing procedures can reduce the buyer's accounting and procurement costs. American Hospital Supply's on-line ordering system for hospitals, for example, allows purchase orders to be placed by less skilled, lower paid clerks instead of purchasing agents. A firm can also provide buyers with advice or technical assistance that reduces their costs. Intel, for example, has a development system to help buyers design its microprocessors cheaply and rapidly into their products. A firm can also take over buyer functions, in effect forward integrating into the buyer's value chain. In wholesaling, for example, Napco stocks shelves, prices goods, and replaces slow-moving items for its buyers.

Table 4–1 Illustrative Product Characteristics that Lower the Buyers' Direct Cost of Use

DIFFERENTIATING FACTOR	EXAMPLE
Reduce usage of the product to achieve an equivalent benefit (including scrap percentage)	Cut-to-size steel sheets
Faster time to process	Quick attaching fasteners
Lower labor costs of use (lower labor inputs, less training, or lower skilled labor required)	Automatic dialers
Reducing quantity of inputs or ancillary equipment required (e.g. fuel, electricity, required shielding from interference, etc.)	Fuel-efficient refrigerator
Lower required maintenance/ spare parts or ease of maintenance	Reliable copiers
Less downtime or idle time	Fast-loading cargo ships
Less required adjustment or monitoring	Uniform-quality paints
Lower failure cost or risk	Blowout preventers for oil wells
Lower installation costs	Single-ply roofing material
Less incoming inspection required	Semiconductors
More rapid setup time	Programmable machine tools
Faster processing time	Tailored aluminum alloys
Reduced risk of damage of other products	Filtration equipment
Higher trade-in value	Durable cars
Compatibility with more types of ancillary equipment	Personal computers

A number of more extended examples will illustrate how firms have lowered their buyers' costs and achieved differentiation. Kodak's copiers, described earlier, lower the buyer's cost of making collated and stapled copies. The industry leader Xerox was more concerned with copying speed itself, which failed to recognize the buyer's full cost of using copiers. In the moving industry, Bekins has offered guaranteed pickup and delivery dates, a fixed price for a move that is quoted in advance, a $100 late payment to the buyer if the move does not occur on time, and reimbursement for damaged goods based on their replacement cost instead of the purchase price. All these lower the buyer's direct and indirect cost of a move (and increase peace of mind as well). In fasteners, Velcro uses a system involving many small plastic hooks that connect to a fibrous pad. Velcro fasteners are easier to install than other forms of fastening devices and eliminate the need for skilled labor in the fastening steps on the buyer's assembly line.

In seeking opportunities to lower buyer costs, a firm must chart in detail how its product moves through or affects the buyer's value chain, including the buyer's inventory, handling, technology development, and administrative activities. It must also be familiar with all other products or inputs its product is used with, and understand how its product interfaces with them. The firm must also identify every other value activity in its value chain that affects the buyer's chain.

Raising Buyer Performance. Raising buyer performance will depend on understanding what is desirable performance from the buyer's viewpoint. Raising the performance of industrial, commercial, and institutional buyer depends on what creates differentiation with their buyers. Thus the needs of the buyer's buyer must be understood, requiring the same analysis as the analysis of buyer value. A truck sold to a buyer who is a consumer goods company that uses it to carry goods to retail stores provides an example. If the retail stores desire frequent deliveries, the consumer goods company will be very interested in a truck with carrying capacity to make frequent deliveries at reasonable cost. Similarly, in selling to automobile manufacturers Velcro achieves differentiation because its fasteners are more flexible and allow interior design options for cars that are appreciated by consumers.

Raising performance of industrial, commercial, or institutional buyers can also be based on helping them meet their noneconomic goals such as status, image, or prestige. In heavy trucks, for example, PACCAR has achieved a high level of differentiation for its Kenworth "K-Whopper" trucks by careful handcrafting and by tailoring them to individual owner specifications. These have little to do with the economic performance of the truck. However, many Kenworth buyers are owner-operators who derive value from the appearance and brand image of their trucks.

For products sold to consumers, raising buyer performance will be a function of better satisfying needs. American Express traveler's checks are used in a stream of consumer activities in which cash needs are irregular, travel plans change, banks are not always available, and a risk of theft or loss exists. American Express differentiates itself because its buyers value the security of redemption anywhere as well as rapid replacement of lost checks. American Express provides easy redemption anywhere via many offices throughout the world that operate long hours.

Conducting the Packaging Analysis

Once the real-world cost of ownership analysis has been completed, the next step in the pricing strategy analysis is to conduct a packaging analysis. The packaging analysis allows the product manager to explore alternative ways to package the product.

To conduct the packaging analysis, add the following seven columns at the top of the product and gross margin analysis spreadsheet. Highlight the header of the columns in a different color than the columns used in the product and gross margin analysis, then copy the pricing data in columns 3 – 9 from the product and gross margin analysis into the seven new columns.

1. New List Price
2. New BOM (Bill of Materials)
3. New COGS (Cost of Goods Sold) The equation should equal BOM + burden cost
4. New Product Margin – The equation should equal 1–(COGS/New List Price)
5. Average Discount – Ask the finance department or use the highest channel partner discount.
6. New Gross Margin = 1–(COGS/(New List Price * (1–Average Discount)))
7. New NET Price = New List Price * (1–Average Discount)

The new seven columns is the packaging analysis. It is where the product manager can strategize on new pricing and packaging strategies.

For example, if the outcome of the product and gross margin analysis showed the product margins were too low to achieve healthy gross margins, raise the prices in the "New List Price" column until they reach the healthy gross margin range. This will give the product manager a clear visual on what the product margins should be to achieve healthy gross margins. Alternatively, if the gross margins are higher than the industry range, then the product manager must assess the overall performance of the product to determine if he or she is asking for too big of a premium. Are sales sluggish or robust? If they are robust, there is no requirement to change. On the other hand, if sales were sluggish, it would be a clear indication that the product is overpriced. Is the product losing market share to competitors? Again, if a loss in market share does not exist, then there is no requirement to change, but if the product is losing market share, then the product manager needs to determine if price is the contributing factor since other factors could be the cause of the loss. For example, the loss in market share is the result of a competitor offering a low-end solution where the product can no longer compete; therefore, the product manager should look at product line extension instead of lowering the price. Can a promotion solve the problem in the short-run? Typically, when there is pricing pressure in the market, the best approach is to use promotions instead of decreasing the price. Is the product's differentiation uniquely able to create competitive advantage for buyers? If this still holds true, then there is no requirement to change, however if the product has been upstaged or matched by the competition in creating competitive advantage for buyers, then lowering the price is definitely on the table, but the product manager should consider all the contributing factors before making a pricing decision. No matter what, product managers should not simply raise or lower prices until he or she has decided on the best pricing and packaging strategy for the product.

Another approach the product manager can take in the packaging analysis is to strategize with the BOM. Examine it closely to determine if changes are required. Specifically, the product manager should examine both the configuration and the cost of the BOM. When examining the configuration of the BOM the major objective is to identify the most convenient way for buyers to purchase the product; fittingly, only what is required to meet the buyer's requirements should be in the BOM. Any add-ons should be optional unless a common purchase configuration exist for buyers. For example, a common purchase configuration for storage arrays includes both Fibre channel and Ethernet network interfaces.

Additionally, the product manager should identify ways to lower manufacturing and BOM costs, but sometimes there has to be a trade-off. For example, I once held the role as a product manager for an ATM (asynchronous transfer mode) Broadband Switch that was close to launch, but the dynamics in the ATM switch market had changed. There was an industry battle between ATM and IP as the preferred networking platform and Fore Systems had announced an aggressive go-to-market strategy for its next generation of ATM switches at a lower price point. As a result, I was compelled to conduct a pricing strategy analysis for the ATM switch to determine its competitiveness in the current market. One aspect of the ATM switch that required scrutiny was the optional traffic shaper daughter-card that attaches to each line card. Because the traffic shaper daughter-card was optional, its manufacturing process was separate from the lines cards, so there were additional manufacturing costs when ordered by the buyer. Therefore, after conferring with the program team, it was determined that the best packaging strategy for the ATM switch would be to build each line card with the traffic shaper daughter-card and have engineering implement the option for traffic shaping in the software. While this would increase the BOM for each line card, I had determined that the increase to the BOM would be significantly less costly than the manufacturing costs to build and assemble the traffic shaper daughter-card separately, since the majority of buyers in our target market would implement the traffic-shaping feature.

Another objective when examining the cost of the BOM is to determine if alternative materials are available to reduce the cost of the BOM, but the product manager must be careful when making changes since there may be consequences that might impact the quality or performance of the product. No matter what, because technology is constantly creating new materials, examining the cost of the BOM should occur on a regular basis.

The packaging analysis allows the product manager to become intimate with different pricing strategies that may be applicable to their product. If the product manager is unfamiliar with different models of pricing, there are many books available written specifically on the topic of pricing strategy. In any case, because pricing strategies are so specific to each product, I will not cover them in this book. The purpose of this book is to help the reader understand how to avoid common mistakes that defeat whichever pricing strategy the product manager employs.

Michael Porter on Pitfalls in Cost Leadership Strategies[5]

Many firms do not fully understand the behavior of their costs from a strategic perspective and fail to exploit opportunities to improve their relative cost position. Some of the most common errors made by firms in assessing and acting upon cost position include:

Exclusive Focus on the Cost of Manufacturing Activities. When one mentions "cost," most managers instinctively think of manufacturing. However, a significant, if not overwhelming, share of total cost is generated in activities such as marketing, sales, service, technology development, and infrastructure. These often receive too little attention in cost analysis. An examination of the entire value chain often results in relatively simple steps that can significantly reduce cost position. For example, recent advances in computers and computer-aided design are having dramatic impacts on the cost of performing research.

Ignoring Procurement. Many firms work diligently to reduce labor costs but pay scant attention to purchased inputs. They tend to view purchasing as a secondary staff function and devote few management resources to it. Analysis within the purchasing department too often centers solely on the purchase price of key raw materials. Firms often allow many items to be purchased by individuals with little expertise or motivation to reduce cost. Linkages between purchased inputs and the costs of other value activities go unrecognized. Modest changes in purchasing practices could yield major cost benefits for many firms.

Overlooking Indirect or Small Activities. Cost reduction programs usually concentrate on large cost activities and/or direct activities such as component fabrication and assembly. Activities that represent a small fraction of total cost seldom receive sufficient scrutiny. Indirect activities, such as maintenance and regulatory costs, often escape attention altogether.

False Perception of Cost Drivers. Firms often misdiagnose their cost drivers. For example, a firm with the largest national market share and the lowest costs may incorrectly assume that national market share drives cost. However, cost leadership may actually stem from the firm's large regional share in the regions in which it operates. Failing to understand the sources of its cost advantage may lead the firm to attempt to lower cost by raising national share. As a result it may worsen its cost position by reducing regional focus. It may also concentrate its defensive strategies on national competitors and ignore the more significant threat posed by strong regional competitors.

Failure to Exploit Linkages. Firms rarely recognize all the linkages that affect cost, particularly linkages with suppliers and linkages among activities such as quality assurance, inspection, and service. Matsushita and Canon, among others, recognize and exploit linkages despite the fact that their policies contradict traditional manufacturing and purchasing practices. Failure to recognize linkages also leads to such errors as requiring each department to cut costs by the same amount, even though *raising* cost in some departments may lower total costs.

Contradictory Cost Reduction. Firms often attempt to reduce cost in ways that are contradictory. They try to gain market share to reap the benefits of scale economies while at the same time dissipating scale economies through model proliferation. They locate close to buyers to save freight costs but emphasize weight reduction in new product development. Cost drivers sometimes work in opposite directions, and a firm must recognize the trade-offs.

Unwitting Cross Subsidy. Firms often engage in unwitting cross subsidy when they fail to recognize the existence of segments in which costs behave differently. Conventional accounting systems rarely measure all the cost differences among products, buyers, channels, or geographic areas described above. Thus, a firm may charge excessive prices on some items in the line or to some buyers while subsidizing prices charged on others. For example, white wine requires less costly cooperage than red wine because of its lower aging requirements. If a winery sets equal prices for white and red wine based on average costs, then the price of lower-cost white wine will subsidize the price of red wine. Unwitting cross subsidy often provides an opening for competitors that understand costs and use them to undercut a firm's prices and improve their market position. Cross subsidy also exposes the firm to focused competitors that only compete in the overpriced segments.

Thinking Incrementally. Cost reduction efforts often strive for incremental cost improvements in the existing value chain, rather than finding ways to reconfigure the chain. Incremental improvement can reach the point of diminishing returns, while reconfiguring the chain can lead to a whole new cost plateau.

Undermining Differentiation. Cost reduction can undermine differentiation if it eliminates a firm's sources of uniqueness to the buyer. Though doing so may be strategically desirable, it should be the result of a conscious choice. Cost reduction efforts should concentrate most on activities that do not contribute to a firm's differentiation. A cost leader will improve performance, moreover, if it differentiates in activities wherever differentiation is not costly. 🙶

How to Review the Pricing Strategy

In this section, I will walk you through the five-step approach I use to review a pricing strategy. The five steps are as follows:

- The Business Case for Changing the Pricing Strategy
- The Complexity of the Pricing Strategy
- The Impact on Suppliers and Channel Partners
- Hidden Costs Passed on to the Customer
- How to Get Approval to Change the Pricing Strategy

The Business Case for Changing the Pricing Strategy

The first step is to review whether there is a business case for changing the pricing strategy. Let me be clear, changing a pricing strategy does not equate to raising or lowering the price of a product. It is taking a holistic view of the product and the dynamics of the market where the product sells to determine the best approach to reach buyers at a premium price.

For example, my first product as a product manager was an integrated router card that ran inside a big network switch, also known as a multiplexer. It was a very troubled product, but I was asked by the Vice President of Marketing to bring it back to life. Specifically, there were six major problems with the product:

1. The product development cycle was two years behind, so the momentum in the sales organization was gone.
2. The performance for the next release of the product would be less than planned.
3. The size of the software running on the integrated router card was a contributing factor for the lower than expected performance. By size, I mean the software was only sold as a single license package that included all eight routed protocols—IP (Internet Protocol), Novell IPX, Open Standards Institute network routing protocol (OSI), DECnet, AppleTalk, Banyan Vines, Apollo Domain, and Xerox Network System (XNS).
4. Through market research and customer feedback, I learned that the majority of my customers only used two of the

routed protocols, the Internet Protocol (IP) and Novell IPX, while a small minority of customers used more.

5. The sales order process for the product was extremely confusing; it had 88 part numbers.

6. The price set for the next release of the product was three times the value for the actual performance the product could deliver.

Therefore, it was evident that I needed to do more than just lower the price of the product because of the performance issue. I needed to take into account all the relevant issues that were wrong with the product—the lack of sales momentum, unattractiveness of the product to the buyer, the complexity of the sales order process, and the overvalued price of the product.

This became the foundation for my business case to change the pricing strategy. To gain sales momentum, I needed to make the product attractive to buyers by changing the packaging, simplifying the sales order process, and correcting the overvalued price of the product.

To make the packaging attractive, I offered two software license packages instead of one: a Base Routing and a Global Routing package. The Base routing package included IP and IPX routed protocols, which the majority of my customers only used, while the Global Routing package included seven of the eight routed protocols; the OSI protocol was removed to achieve better performance. To simplify the sales order process, I reduced the 88 part numbers down to thirty-five; twenty for the product and fifteen for the upgrades. Lastly, to correct the overvalued pricing of the product, I changed the pricing to represent the actual performance and value of the product, which required renegotiating the OEM software license's royalties to achieve healthy gross margins. As a result, the new packaging and pricing strategy achieved an increase in revenue by 77 percent and 91 percent, sequentially.

Before the product manager changes a pricing strategy, he or she should take a holistic view of the product and the buyers' requirements to understand all the relevant issues that are wrong with the product. It does not have to be a performance problem. It could be a weakness or slowdown in sales, the entrance of a new competitor, an economic downturn, or even product line extension can cause problems for a product. For example, a product manager in the application software industry has product margins above 84% and gross margins above 72%, which is in the range of healthy gross margins, but over the past few quarters product sales have significantly declined. This would be an indication that the dynamics of the market have changed. The call to action for the product manager is to identify the cause for the weakness in sales and determine if there is a business case to change the pricing strategy.

Additionally, if the results of a real world cost of ownership analysis reveal competitive advantages that were previously unknown, the product manager should evaluate if the current pricing strategy aligns with any new positioning he or she is using to articulate those competitive advantages. Specifically, if a product sits at the low end of the range for healthy gross margins and the product manager uncovers new competitive advantages, serious consideration to raise the product margins should be given.

Although it will not be a popular decision with the sales organization, failure to price in the competitive advantages will diminish the value the product provides; moreover, there could be consequences in the future. For example, if an economic downturn occurs and the product manager did not price in the competitive advantages, he or she will quickly realize the potential profits are forever gone. Alternatively, if the product manager is not comfortable pricing in the competitive advantages, at the very least create a test market or conduct a focus group to confirm the strength of the competitive advantages the product is creating for its buyers.

Overall, my recommendation for product managers is to review the pricing strategy on a regular basis. The dynamics of markets change and with every release of the product there will also be change. Regardless, product managers should not rush these analyses, but spend time understanding the packaging and the pricing strategy of the product, so when the time comes to make a change they will be better prepared to make their business case.

The Complexity of the Pricing Strategy

The second step is to review the complexity of the pricing strategy. Specifically, the product manager should review the complexity of the pricing strategy in the sales order process, in product line extension, and in bundling.

Sales Order Process. Is the sales order process for the product too complex or confusing for buyers? This is an important question for the product manager to answer because complex or confusing pricing will diminish the value of a product. It will also slow down the close process because the buyer will not purchase without clarity. Keep in mind that in most cases high-tech products are large purchases. In fact, most buyers consider them an investment; therefore, buyers take a purchase decision very seriously. Typically, pricing is not presented to a buyer until the close of a deal; as a result, even though the account manager has gone through all the stages of selling to get the buyer to that point, there will always be some apprehension by the buyer when she or he is presented with the purchase order. If the pricing is not straightforward and easy to understand, all the efforts of the account manager will have been in vain, and the buyer's level of resistance to make the purchase will rise, as will their expectation for a higher discount. Complex or confusing sales order processes makes it easier for the buyer to change her or his mind.

Throughout my career, I have seen a lot of complex and confusing pricing, but the most profound pricing I have ever seen was a software product that had exact opposite pricing strategies by the licenser and an OEM. Specifically, the OEM sold the software using a razor and blade pricing strategy, while the licenser sold the software using a pricing strategy that was the exact opposite; they sold the base software license at a high price and each additional tier of the software license at a low price. Consequently, since both companies were selling the software through channel partners, when the channel partners representing the two companies competed on the same deal, the buyer became very confused. The buyer understood it was the same software, but figuring out which offer was the better deal was problematic, since the pricing strategies were opposite to each other. Rightly, it was harder for the buyer to make a purchase decision, which is not what either company wanted a buyer to experience. To make a long story short, the licenser decided to change the pricing strategy to match the razor and blade pricing strategy used by the OEM in order to prevent any further confusion for buyers. For this reason, product managers who sell through OEMs should take the time to understand their OEM's pricing strategy. While it seems uncanny that this could happen, it did, and so the possibility is there that it could happen to other companies.

Product Line Extension and Bundling. Another area to look for complexity in the pricing strategy is product line extension. In particular, the product manager should examine whether she or he is offering too many options of the product and if any of the product options is cannibalizing the sales of the core product. In general, product line extension happens because the product manager wants to go after competitors that are at the low end or high end of where the core product sits in the market. On the other hand, if the product line's market share is not growing because of product line extension, then some of the product options are cannibalizing the sales of the core product. Often this occurs at the low end of the market, so profits are being lost. For this reason, the product manager must find a way to re-establish value for the core product. In addition, if any of the product options in the product line are poor performers, it would be wise for the product manager to evaluate whether he or she should keep them active in the product line; the poor performers are not creating competitive advantages for many buyers, and it is costly for the company to continue producing them.

Likewise, the product manager should look for opportunities where bundling would reduce complexity in the pricing strategy. Buyers will appreciate the simplicity bundling provides, but the bundle has to make sense from the buyer's perspective. It has to meet the buyer's need and express a value for the buyer in purchasing it. The overall objective when bundling products is to make the bundle more attractive than purchasing the products or items separately. In Chapter 3, I will discuss bundling in detail.

The complexity of the pricing strategy can diminish the value of a product if the product manager does not address the issues. One way to determine if there is a problem is to solicit feedback from buyers and the sales organization. An account manager once told me on the day he resigned from the company where we worked, that his reason for leaving was that it was just too difficult to do business with the company. Hence, if an account manager is dissatisfied with the complexity of the pricing strategy, then the buyer will be dissatisfied as well. Fittingly, it is very important for product managers to review the pricing and packaging strategies, to remove as much complexity as possible. In Chapter 3, I will provide further discussion on the attractiveness of packaging.

The Impact on Suppliers and Channel Partners

The third step is to review the impact a pricing strategy change will have on suppliers and channel partners. It could affect the amount of compensation a supplier or channel partner earns from the sales of a product. For example, if a change in the pricing strategy negatively affects a supplier, such as a decline in the use of a supplier's product, it could cause the supplier to raise its prices to recapture the value creation it would lose. Alternatively, in some instances like the semiconductor industry, if the volume is not sufficient it could cause them to stop production all together. Likewise, if a change in the pricing strategy negatively affects a channel partner, it could cause the channel partner to place less focus on selling the product or seek alternatives.

On the other hand, a change in the pricing strategy could benefit suppliers and channel partners if the change to a pricing strategy improves the sales of the product. For example, when the licenser mentioned above changed the pricing strategy to match the OEM's razor and blade pricing strategy, the channel partners benefited because the software price was competitive and the confusion from the opposite pricing strategy no longer existed. What is more, because the razor and blade pricing strategy allowed the channel partners to charge a lower entry price for the base software license, and then recover the margin from the sale of additional tiers of the software license, the licenser was able to convince the channel partners to allow them to lower their channel discount. It was a win-win for everyone involved, the buyer, the channel partners, and the licenser. Therefore, it is important to understand the impact on channel partners before changing the pricing strategy. The outcome may conclude that no change in discount is required. On the other hand, the outcome might require increasing or decreasing the channel partner discount depending on the pricing strategy the product manager chooses to employ.

Additionally, the product manager should take into account any spiffs or market development funds the sales and marketing departments are giving to channel partners. In most instances, spiffs and market development funds are directly tied to a specific product or product line. Therefore, if spiffs or market development funds are not being offered for the product, the product manager should evaluate whether to use them in constructing the channel partner discount strategy when changing the pricing strategy.

Michael Porter on Vertical Linkages[6]

Linkages exist not only within a firm's value chain but between a firm's chain and the value chains of suppliers and channels. These linkages, which I term vertical linkages, are similar to the linkages within the value chain—the way supplier or channel activities are performed affects the cost or performance of a firm's activities (and vice versa). Suppliers produce a product or service that a firm employs in its value chain, and the suppliers' value chain also influence the firm at other contact points. A firm's procurement and inbound logistics activities interact with a supplier's order entry system, for example, while a supplier's applications engineering staff works with a firm's technology department and manufacturing activities. A supplier's product characteristics as well as its other contact points with a firm's value chain can significantly affect a firm's cost and differentiation. For example, frequent supplier shipments can reduce a firm's inventory needs, appropriate packaging of supplier products can lower handling cost, and supplier inspection can remove the need for incoming inspection by a firm.

The linkages between suppliers' value chains and a firm's value chain provide opportunities for the firm to enhance its competitive advantage. It is often possible to benefit both the firm and suppliers by influencing the configuration of suppliers' value chains to jointly optimize the performance of activities, or by improving coordination between a firm's and suppliers' chains. Supplier linkages mean that the relationship with suppliers is *not a zero sum* game in which one gains only at the expense of the other, but a relationship in which both can gain. By agreeing to deliver bulk chocolate to a confectionery producer in tank cars instead of solid bars, for example, an industrial chocolate firm saves the cost of molding and packaging while the confectionery manufacturer lowers the cost of in-bound handling and melting. The division of the benefits of coordinating or optimizing linkages between a firm and its suppliers is a function of supplier's bargaining power and is reflected in suppliers' margins. Supplier bargaining power is partly structural and partly a function of a firm's purchasing practices. Thus, *both* coordination with suppliers and hard bargaining to capture the spoils are important to competitive advantage. One without the other results in missed opportunities.

Channel linkages are similar to supplier linkages. Channels have value chains through which a firm's product passes. The channel markup over a firm's selling price (which I term channel value) often represents a large proportion of the selling price to the end user—it represents as much as 50 percent or more of selling price to the end user in many consumer goods, such as wine. Channels perform such activities as sales, advertising, and display that may substitute for or complement the firm's activities. There are also multiple points of contact between a firm's and channel's value chains in activities such as the sales force, order entry, and out-bound logistics. As with supplier linkages, coordinating and jointly optimizing with channels can lower cost or enhance differentiation. The same issues that existed with suppliers in dividing the gains of coordination and joint optimization also exist with channels.

Vertical linkages, like linkages within a firm's value chain, are frequently overlooked. Even if they are recognized, independent ownership of suppliers or channels or a history of an adversary relationship can impede the coordination and joint optimization required to exploit vertical linkages. Sometimes vertical linkages are easier to achieve with coalition partners or sister business units than with independent firms, though even this is not assured. As with linkages within the value chain, exploiting vertical linkages requires information and modern information systems are creating many new possibilities. ""

Hidden Costs Passed On to the Customer

The fourth step is to review the hidden costs associated with the purchase of the product. Typically, this happens when a product does not provide a complete solution that forces the buyer to spend more time and money than anticipated to create the complete solution. The more time and money spent by the buyer to implement the complete solution will diminish the value of the product. Likewise, it can unglue the product's positioning, if the product manager is making claims that the product lowers cost or reduces time to market.

When hidden costs exist and cannot be reduced or eliminated, the product manager must change the product positioning if claims to lower cost or reduce time to market exist. Failure to do so will cause the company to lose credibility. Additionally, should a competitor realize the inaccuracy of the claim, they will waste no time telling the company's prospects about it.

An alternative and better method to address hidden costs is to offer the complete solution by partnering with other companies or developing the complete solution in-house. For example, a company sells software to OEMs to reduce their time to market, but integrating the software into the OEM's product requires an extensive amount of customization. Some buyers will choose to do it themselves, while others are compelled to purchase professional services. No matter what, the positioning of the software as reducing time to market is not what the OEMs are experiencing because the integration of the software requires an extensive amount of customization. The product manager should have the engineering team design and develop an integration solution for the OEMs that would reduce the time to integrate the software. As a result,even though the integration solution would be an additional expense to the buyer, the hidden costs have been significantly reduced. What is more, the cost for the integration solution would be significantly less than what the cost would be for the buyers to do it themselves. Most importantly, the corrective action by the product manager will enable the positioning of the software as reducing time to market to remain intact.

Hidden costs passed on to buyers are not obvious because they are hidden. Unfortunately, the buyer is typically the first to know. This is why it is important to get feedback from buyers about problems or issues they are experiencing; otherwise, the product manager will see the value of their product diminish, making buyers more reluctant to pay a premium price.

When reviewing the pricing strategy always try to identify any hidden costs. One way to identify them is to conduct the real-world cost of ownership analysis. When comparing the product to the competition, the product manager should look to see if the competition is addressing a hidden cost he or she may have overlooked.

Michael Porter on Competitive Advantages from Controlling Complements[7]

Improve Buyer Performance and Thus Differentiate. Complements often affect the performance of a product or the firm's overall value to the buyer. Well-designed software can improve the performance of a personal computer, just as toner affects the copy quality of plain paper copiers. Similarly, a food concessionaire can significantly affect the buyer's satisfaction with a racetrack. Gaining the performance benefit of controlling complements often requires bundling. A firm that controls a complement may thus be able to enhance differentiation.

A firm gains a competitive advantage in differentiation from controlling complements if competitors do not. Even if control over a complement is widespread in an industry, however, it can still be beneficial if it improves overall industry structure though no firm gains a competitive advantage.

Improve the Perception of Value. Complements frequently affect each other's image or perceived quality. If mobile home parks look shoddy or are poorly designed, for example, this can adversely affect how buyers perceive mobile homes. Because of their association in the buyer's mind, compliments are frequently signaling criteria for each other. Controlling a complement can yield a competitive advantage in signaling even if a firm does not bundle. For example, Kodak's strong position in film improves its perceived differentiation vis- à-vis other camera manufacturers that do not sell film, even though Kodak sells cameras and film separately.

Controlling complements to signal value may be beneficial to industry structure even if no one firm gains a competitive advantage from doing so. In the mobile home industry, for example, the overall image of mobile homes could be improved if all mobile home producers also developed high quality mobile home parks. This would increase the demand for mobile home versus other forms of housing and benefit the entire industry. Control over complements by one firm may, in fact, have little impact on buyer perceptions unless a sufficient number of competitors also control the complement. In these cases a firm should actually work to encourage its competitors to enter the complementary industry along with it.

Optimal Pricing. The buyer's purchase decision is frequently on the total cost of a product and complements, rather than on the cost of the product alone. For example, buyers usually measure the cost of a condominium or automobile by the total monthly payment required (including principal and financing cost), rather than looking solely at the price of the condominium or automobile itself. Similarly, buyers may evaluate the cost of going to a movie in terms of the cost of the movie plus the cost of parking. Under these circumstances, prices must be set jointly to maximize profits, and this is difficult to do without controlling the compliment. When setting the price of parking at a movie theater, one must recognize that lowering the cost of parking may increase the number of movie tickets sold, for example.

As with differentiation, the benefits of controlling a complement for pricing do *not* require that the firm sell the product and complement as a bundle, or even that the firm have a market share in the complement that is comparable to its share of the base product. Even with a relatively small position in the complement, a firm can influence pricing in the complementary industry by initiating pricing moves that competitors are forced (or inclined) to follow. By lowering its own parking prices, for example, a movie theatre firm may be able to force down prices at other parking garages in the area to some extent. Thus a position in the complement gives the firm a leverage point with which to influence the development of the complement's industry, and its position in the complement need only be big enough to allow exercising such leverage.

Reduce Marketing and Selling Cost. Control over complements can lead to economies in marketing, because the demands for a product and for complements are related. Advertising and other marketing investments for one complement often boost demand for the other, and complements may be susceptible to shared marketing or selling. Similarly, an installed base in one product can lower the cost of marketing complements. In video games, for example, an installed base of machines helps the firm sell game cartridges. The economies are sometimes large enough so that a firm not controlling complements is unable to reach the threshold spending on marketing needed to be effective.

A firm gains a cost advantage in marketing if it is one of relatively few firms that controls a complement. Widespread control over complements can benefit the industry as a whole, however, if it raises marketing expenditures and boosts overall industry demand relative to substitute products. Widespread control over complements may also help overcome the "free rider" problem, where firms selling one complement piggyback on the marketing investments of firms selling others. Even if a firm's decision to control a complement is quickly imitated by competitors, such a move will still be beneficial to the industry as a whole.

Sharing Other Activities. Controlling a complement may allow a firm to share other activities in the value chain besides marketing and sales. The same logistical system may be employed to deliver a product and complements, for example, or the same order entry system. Opportunities for sharing will often be present because of the fact that complements are sold to the same buyers.

Raise Mobility Barriers. Where controlling a complement leads to one or more of the competitive advantages described above, it may also increase overall entry/mobility barriers into the industry *if* entry barriers into the complementary product are significant. For example, a real estate developer that could own a bank (and get preferential access to financing) would significantly increase the sustainability of its competitive advantage because the barriers to entry into banking are significant for most real estate developers. Today real estate developers are legally prohibited from owning banks, though deregulation may change this in the future.

The benefits of controlling a complement are not mutually exclusive, and any or all can be present in an industry. For example, the food concession can not only affect the buyer's satisfaction with the racetrack, but prices should be set jointly on concessions and admission. Depending on the characteristics of buyers, low admission prices may well raise the number of patrons who will buy high priced hot dogs. Control over both the racetrack and the food concession can lead at the same time to economies in marketing. The sustainability of the competitive advantage from controlling a complement depends on the presence of some barriers to entering the complementary good. Without them, competitors can readily replicate the advantage through entering the complementary industry themselves.

The benefits of controlling a complement can sometimes be achieved through coalitions with other firms without the need for actual ownership. For example, a firm and the supplier of a complement can agree to coordinate prices, or agree to pool their marketing budgets. The problem with such arrangements is the difficulty of reaching a stable agreement. As long as firms supplying complements are independent, each will be tempted to free-ride on the other, and to set prices and strategies to maximize its profits rather than the joint profits of both. Nevertheless, the possibilities of using coalitions to achieve the benefits of controlling complements must always be explored. If the possibility exists it may be the most cost-effective option for a firm (or for the firm's competitors). Sometimes equity investments or other forms of quasi-integration between a firm and the supplier of a complementary product can overcome the difficulties of coordinating behavior.

How to Get Approval to Change the Pricing Strategy

The fifth step is to review the approval process for changing a pricing strategy. More than likely, because changing a pricing strategy will have an impact on the company's business plan, the product manager will need to get approval from the CEO and agreement by his executive or senior staff. Additionally, if the change to the pricing strategy gets approval, it will have an impact on other departments in the company, so the product manager will need to notify them. The finance and accounting departments will need to know because finance manages the business plan, and accounting tracks the revenue. Sales and sales operations need to know for purposes of forecasting, discounting, and sales commissions. If the new pricing strategy involves changes in the packaging, Marketing must update all the product literature, manufacturing operations must update or create the new BOMs and manufacturer part numbers, and the I.T. department must update all the business systems.

What's more, since most high-tech companies charge for technical support based on a percentage of the list price of the product, the customer support department needs advisement prior to seeking approval for a change in the pricing strategy. The price change will affect their business plan, so notifying them in advance will give them a chance to determine if they need to change the percentage.

Since the services organization provides onsite support, installation services, training, return material authorization (RMA), depot, and technical publications support, they also need to be informed when there is a change in the packaging.

The legal department will need to review the terms and conditions, every customer contract and volume purchase agreement associated with the product, especially if the new pricing strategy involves a change in the product's warranty. The product manager should not overlook this step.

Lastly, the product manager will need to notify every channel partner, distributor, and reseller associated with the product. They need to know as soon as possible, so they can update their price list and notify their sales organization of the change. Additionally, if the packaging changed, distributors might need to order more stock or replace stock to support the new packaging. For example, if the packaging changed to sell the product as a bundle, the distributor may not have sufficient inventory to support the bundle; rightfully, prior to notifying distributors the product manager should identify how much stock the distributors have on hand.

Most importantly, the product manager should not change the prices on the price list until every department has signed off on the change to the pricing strategy. It would be foolish to move forward without it. A department might forget or become distracted and fail to follow through with the necessary changes or updates. As a result, the buyer becomes a victim of the oversight and the value of the product is diminished.

If the company does not have a formal approval process that requires notifying each department, the product manager should make it a point to do it anyway. It will save the product manager many headaches to be proactive. Alternatively, some companies use a pricing committee or council that includes representatives from the different departments. In this situation, the product manager must present the business case for changing the pricing strategy to the committee in order to get approval. Typically, the committee will have the authority to ask the product manager to make changes and come back several times. Therefore, it is best for the product manager to reach out to each member in advance to make sure all his or her bases are covered.

In any event, it is very important for the product manager to understand the approval process because politics are unavoidable when changing a pricing strategy. In all honesty, going through the approval process is no cakewalk. Individuals who once were the product manager's allies quickly will become foes, especially if they think the change will have a negative impact on them. Whether it will or not does not matter. The product manager should also anticipate encounters from overly cautious and conservative people who do not like change, even if it is in the best interest of the product. Then again, others will throw out an unknown issue at the last minute just to get their fifteen minutes of fame; however, the product manager should not worry about those individuals because their fifteen minutes of fame will not be popular with executive management. I recommend anticipating many obstacles.

Emotionally it will make it easier for the product manager to get through the process. The approval process will be personal and emotional for a product manager, since he or she has the most to lose—the success of their product. Furthermore, do not be surprise if there is a lack of overwhelming support up the chain of command as the product manager goes through the process. The chain of command may be distracted by other politics going on at the time and would prefer not to have the drama that comes with changing a pricing strategy.

When I went through the approval process to change the pricing strategy for the integrated router card, the politics were so intense I had to go off topic to defend my business case for changing the pricing strategy. I explained it by equating the integrated router card to a Mercedes Benz with a Chevy Chevette engine inside. In fact, I recommend that every product manager have an off-topic way of defending his or her business case since there is a high probability that others will engage in attempting to sabotage their effort; it is all about being prepared for the obstacles.

The product manager is the CEO of the product; no matter what obstacles are present, it is his or her job to make the product a success. If the product manager has done all the analysis and the business case is solid, the product manager should not let the politics be intimidating.

If allies turn to foes, find new allies by seeking out individuals who will benefit from what he or she is trying to accomplish. Most importantly, whether the individual is an ally or a foe, the product manager should listen to any feedback being offered since someone might know something the product manager is not aware of that can help improve going through the process.

In summary, every product manager should know the pricing strategy of his or her product and review it on a regular basis. The best approach is to conduct a pricing strategy analysis. Start with the product and gross margin analysis. Once the current pricing strategy is set up in the spreadsheet, do the test for healthy gross margins. The next step is to conduct the real-world cost of ownership analysis. It will allow the product manager to identify any unknown competitive advantages or differentiations that translate into creating competitive advantages for buyers. Once the real-world cost of ownership analysis is completed, add the additional seven columns into the spreadsheet to conduct the packaging analysis. Play around with creating new packaging and pricing strategies. Be sure to reference pricing strategy books to identify other pricing strategies that might be suitable for the product. Once the product manager has identified the best pricing strategy, he or she should walk through the five steps I provided for reviewing it.

1. The Business Case for Changing the Pricing Strategy
2. The Complexity of the Pricing Strategy
3. The Impact on Suppliers and Channel Partners
4. Hidden Costs Passed on to the Customer
5. How to Get Approval to Change the Pricing Strategy.

Doing this will provide a strong foundation to finalize a decision on whether a business case exits to change the pricing strategy. Whatever the decision is, do not settle for just changing the price of the product. The product manager should take a holistic approach to understand the product and the dynamics of the market where it sells, so the best pricing strategy can be determined to make buyers less reluctant to pay a premium price.

2 | The Value Isn't Obvious

In the introduction to this book, I gave an example of two companies that have a history of selling products at a premium price, Apple and Cisco. The reason why historically they have been able to do this is that the value of their products was obvious in the positioning. Too often product managers fail to make this connection with buyers, so the buyer does not perceive the actual value of the product. Therefore, refraining from making the value obvious in the positioning diminishes a buyer's willingness to purchase the product at a premium price.

At a high level, there are fundamentally two categories of products: revolutionary products and evolutionary products. Revolutionary products jump to the next generation. The benefits are so significant that change happens in a short period of time and on a large scale. The entire product category transforms. A good example would be the jump to cell phones from landline phones, since the significant benefit of cell phones is mobility; being able to take them anywhere and everywhere you go. On the other hand, evolutionary products take incremental steps to the next generation of products over a long period of time. For example, music players have evolved over the years from the introduction of the phonograph in 1877 to today's small digital devices that fit in your pocket and have the tracks stored in the "cloud." As a result, the approach to making value obvious for a revolutionary product will be different from the approach for making value obvious for an evolutionary product. To that end, I will discuss each category separately in this chapter.

Making Value Obvious with Revolutionary Products

For a product to be categorized as revolutionary, it has to provide a significant benefit to buyers that make them willing to change. In some industries that does not come easily. For example, getting large enterprise companies in the financial industry to transition to a new technology is extremely difficult because the data centers and networks of financial institutions are mission critical and require more than five nines (.99999) availability. Hence, financial institutions are conservative in transitioning to new technology.

For these reasons, a revolutionary product would have to provide tremendous value for a financial institution to disrupt the way they do business. The transition is disruptive because revolutionary products are disruptive. They are about a dramatic change in the way a company conducts business. The buyer's experience is going to be significantly different, and the change will be highly beneficial. For example, the storage industry currently is going through a revolutionary change from hard disk drive (HDD) storage arrays to solid-state drive (SSD) storage arrays in data centers. Hard disk drives (HDD) storage arrays use electromechanical magnetic disks while solid-state drive (SSD) storage arrays use flash memory. In any case, solid-state drive (SSD) storage arrays offer superior performance over hard disk drive (HDD) storage arrays; however, buyers have been reluctant to purchase solid-state drive (SSD) storage arrays because they are perceived to be very expensive compared to hard disk drive (HDD) storage arrays, seven to eight times more expensive per unit of storage.

What this indicates is that the value in the positioning of solid-state drive (SSD) storage arrays is not obvious to buyers. Even though superior performance is a good differentiator between the two technologies, it does not articulate the competitive advantage solid-state drive (SSD) storage arrays create for its buyers that would make them less reluctant to pay a premium price. In other words, it is not as if every company can justify buying a Lear Jet, but if purchasing the Lear Jet will provide cost savings or increase productivity, they definitely would be less reluctant to pay a premium price.

Facing this dilemma, a real world cost of ownership analysis was conducted by IBM that compared the two technologies. The result of the analysis identified that the competitive advantage solid-state drive (SSD) storage arrays create for its buyers is CAPEX and OPEX savings. Specifically, to improve the performance of hard disk drive (HDD) storage arrays buyers would have to limit the storage capacity on hard disk drive (HDD) storage arrays by 20% to 50%, but with solid-state drive (SSD) storage arrays buyers would get superior performance using close to 100% of the storage capacity. This translates into a reduced footprint, e.g., floor space and lower energy costs because the buyer can replace many hard disk drive (HDD) storage arrays with only a few solid-state drive (SSD) storage arrays.[8] Product managers for solid-state drive (SSD) storage arrays need to make the value obvious in the positioning of their products by communicating how solid-state drive (SSD) storage arrays lower buyer costs.

Similarly, the information technology industry is going through a revolutionary change from collaboration tools over the PSTN (public switched telephone network) to collaboration tools over Internet and IP networks. Specifically, from the use of phones, voice mail, email, video conferencing, and group support systems over the PSTN (public switched telephone network) to voice, video, instant messaging, web conferencing, and web collaboration over the Internet and IP networks. In any case, because it is harder to measure increased productivity as opposed to lowering buyer cost, which is what collaboration products do, buyers have been more reluctant to pay a premium price. Product managers for collaboration products need to make the value obvious in the positioning of their products by articulating how collaboration tools create competitive advantages for their buyers by raising the buyer's performance. This can be accomplished by conducting a real-world cost of ownership analysis that compares collaboration tools over the PSTN to collaboration tools over the Internet and IP networks to identify the competitive advantages or translate the differentiation into creating competitive advantages for their buyers. For example, mobility options are far more advanced today over the Internet and IP networks than they are over the PSTN. Mobile versions of collaboration tools can be installed on smartphones, tablets, and laptops to enable access to web collaboration tools such as Cisco's WebEx and Microsoft's Skype and Lync for video conferencing, online meetings, instant messaging, and voice over the Internet and IP networks. Thus, allowing users to access collaboration tools from anywhere and everywhere they go, which will greatly improve the buyer's productivity.

To summarize, product managers of revolutionary products should conduct a real-world cost of ownership analysis to compare the current generation product to the next generation product. The goal is to identify what competitive advantages the product creates for its buyers or to translate how the product's differentiation uniquely creates competitive advantages for its buyers by lowering the buyer's costs or raising the buyer's performance. When conducting a real-world cost of ownership analysis, the product manager should use only one application for the product. This will make the differentiation very clear in the model, but if the product manager feels she or he must cover every application, then a real-world cost of ownership analysis should be conducted for each application separately. Typically, a competitive advantage reduces costs, gains efficiency, increases revenue, improves productivity, or reduces time to market.

Product managers should not get caught in the differentiation trap of only positioning their product by using words that do not establish real value for the buyer such as superior performance, a compact size, scalability, etc. The value is not obvious when differentiation is used in that manner. For a product to be a successful, the product manager needs to create competitive advantages for its buyers and make the value obvious in the positioning of the product by communicating how the product will lower the buyer's costs or raise the buyer's performance.

Making Value Obvious with Evolutionary Products

Making the value obvious for an evolutionary product involves a different set of circumstances than for a revolutionary product. Product managers of revolutionary products should conduct a real-world cost of ownership analysis that compares the current generation product to the next generation product to identify the competitive advantages. On the other hand, with an evolutionary product the product manager should conduct the real-world cost of ownership analysis to compare the product against the competition. Let us take a closer look at making value obvious for an evolutionary product.

Typically, an evolutionary product has been in the market for several years and has experienced tremendous success. Moreover, during this time new features have been added to enhance the product and it has gone through a couple of redesigns; however, along with the success came competitors with "me too" products that use feature differentiation to establish value such as speed, density, form factor, or architecture. Unfortunately, product managers of "me too" products rarely make the effort to establish what competitive advantages their product creates for their buyers because they are riding the on coat tail of the competitive advantages established by the original innovator of the product category. As a result, the value is not obvious because the positioning is based on feature differentiation that has not been translated into creating competitive advantages for the buyer by either lowering the buyer's costs or raising the buyer's performance. Fittingly, "me too" products tend to drag the value down for all products in the product category due to increased price competition.

For example, in Chapter 1 I wrote about my experience conducting a real-world cost of ownership analysis for an edge-router sold to service providers. It was a new "me too" product that competed against other edge-routers already in the product category. What made this edge-router different from its competitors was the architecture. It had both a modular hardware and software architecture in a smaller footprint that provided five nines (.99999) availability, higher throughput and performance, and a higher capacity of ports. As a result, because of the strong feature differentiation it was evident that the engineers had built a better edge-router even though the edge-router was sold at a lower price than all its competitors, which was contradictory given the strong feature differentiation. What is more, because the value was not obvious in the positioning of the edge-router, buyers had been more reluctant to pay a premium price. They could not see the actual value of the product due to the use of feature differentiation in the positioning of the edge-router instead of communicating how the product would lower the buyer's costs or increase the buyer's performance, which led the product manager to compete on price. The product manager was riding on the coattail of the competitive advantages that the original edge-router created for its buyers. What's more, in the telecommunications industry a price advantage rarely works. The majority of service providers do not buy products based on price. They buy products to solve their problems, so making the value obvious is far more important than competing on price. Fortunately, the real-world cost of ownership analysis I conducted revealed that the edge-router created competitive advantages for its buyers in CAPEX and OPEX savings over the competition. In other words, the service provider edge-router would lower the buyer's costs. As a result, the product manager was able to make the value obvious for the edge-router, so buyers were less reluctant to pay a premium price.

What every product manager needs to understand is that differentiation alone does not express the full value of the product, but translating the product's differentiation into creating competitive advantages for buyers will. For this reason, it is important for the product manager to translate the differentiation into creating competitive advantages for his or her buyers by communicating how the product would lower the buyer's costs or raise the buyer's performance. On the other hand, if the differentiation cannot be translated into creating competitive advantages for the buyer, then the product manager should leverage competitive advantages the company creates for its buyers, which I will discuss later in this chapter.

To summarize, product managers of evolutionary products should conduct a real-world cost of ownership analysis to compare the product against the competition. The goal is to identify what competitive advantages the product creates for its buyers or translate how the product's differentiation creates competitive advantages for its buyers by either lowering the buyer's costs or raising the buyer's performance. When conducting a real-world cost of ownership analysis, the product manager should use only one application of the product or do each application separately. This will make the differentiation very clear in the model. Typically, a competitive advantage reduces costs, gains efficiency, increases revenue, improves productivity, or reduces time to market. Again, product managers should not get caught in the differentiation trap of only positioning their product by using words that do not establish real value for the buyer such as superior performance, a compact size, scalability, etc. The value is not obvious when differentiation is used in that manner. For a product to be a successful, the product manager needs to create competitive advantages for its buyer and make the value obvious in the positioning of the product by communicating how the product will lower the buyer's costs or raise the buyer's performance.

Michael Porter on Identifying Purchase Criteria[9]

Identification of purchase criteria begins by identifying the decision maker for a firm's product and the other individuals that influence the decision maker. The channels may be an intermediate buyer that must be analyzed as well. Use criteria should be identified first, because they measure the sources of buyer value and also often determine signaling criteria. A number of parallel approaches should be employed to identify use criteria. Internal knowledge of the buyer's needs constitutes an initial source of use criteria. However, conventional wisdom may color internal perception of use criteria; an internal analysis alone is insufficient. No analysis of buyer purchase criteria should ever be accepted unless it includes some direct contact with the buyer. However, even talking to buyers, as essential as it is, is insufficient because buyers often do not fully understand all the ways in which a firm can affect their cost or performance and they may also not tell the truth. In any serious effort to understand buyer purchase criteria, then, a firm must identify the buyer's value chain and perform a systematic analysis of all existing and potential linkages between a firm's value chain and its buyer's chain. This sort of analysis can not only uncover unrecognized use criteria, but also show how to assess the relative weight of well-known use criteria.

Use criteria must be identified *precisely* in order to be meaningful for developing differentiation strategy. Many firms speak of their buyers' use criteria in vague terms such as "high quality" or "delivery." At this level of generality, a firm cannot begin to calculate the value of meeting a use criterion to the buyer, nor can the firm know how to change its behavior to increase buyer value. Quality could mean higher specifications or better conformance, for example. For McDonald's, consistency of hamburger and french fry quality over time and across locations is important as is taste and portion size. Improving these two things involves very different actions by a firm. Service can also mean many things, including backing of claims, repair capability, response time to service requests, and delivery time.

Good performance in meeting each use criteria should be quantified if possible. For example, the quality of a food ingredient might be measured in terms of the particle count of extraneous material or the percentage of fat content. Quantification not only forces careful thinking to determine what precisely the buyer values, but also allows the measurement and tracking of firm performance against a use criterion—this often yields major improvements in performance in and of itself. Quantification also allows a firm to assess its position against competitors in meeting important criteria. The firm can then study the practices that underlie competitors' performance.

A firm can calculate the value of meeting each use criterion by estimating how it affects the buyer's cost or performance. Such calculations inevitably involve judgments, but are an indispensable tool in choosing a sustainable differentiation strategy. Determining the buyer value in meeting each use criterion will allow them to be ranked in order of importance. For some use criteria a firm must only meet a threshold value to satisfy the buyer's need, while for others more performance against them is always better. If a TV set warms up in two seconds, for example, there is little additional benefit if the time is reduced to one second. Nearly all use criteria will reach a point of diminishing returns, however, after which further improvement is not valuable or will actually *reduce* buyer value. Meeting some use criteria may also involve trade-offs with others. Calculating the buyer value from meeting each use criterion will illuminate the relevant thresholds, trade-offs, and buyer value that accrues to additional improvement in meeting it. A firm can only make its own assessments of the balance between the value of differentiation and its cost if it understands these things. The ranking of use criteria in terms of the buyer value of meeting them will often contradict conventional wisdom.

Signaling criteria can be identified by understanding the process the buyer uses to form judgments about a firm's potential ability to meet use criteria, as well as how well it is actually meeting them. Examining each use criteria to determine possible signals is a good place to start. If a key use criterion is reliability of delivery, for example, past delivery record and customer testimonials might be signals of value. Two other analytical steps can also provide insight into signals of value. By carefully analyzing the *process by which the buyer purchases*, including the information sources consulted, the testing or inspection procedures carried out, and the steps in reaching the decision, signals of value may become apparent. This sort of analysis will yield indications about what a buyer consults or notices, including channels. A related way of identifying signaling criteria is to identify *significant points of contact* between a firm and the buyer both before and after purchase, including the channels, trade shows, accounting department, and others. Every point of contact represents an opportunity to influence the buyer's perception of a firm and thus is a possible signaling criterion.

Like use criteria, signaling criteria should be defined as precisely and operationally as possible in order to guide differentiation strategy. In a bank, for example the appearance of facilities can signal value through its order, permanence, and security. For a designer clothing store, other dimensions of appearance would be more appropriate. Signaling criteria vary in importance, and a firm must rank them in terms of their impact on buyer perception in order to make choices about how much to spend on them. Calculating the contribution of signaling criteria to realize price is often difficult, but focus groups and interviews may be helpful. As with use criteria, meeting signaling criteria can reach the point of diminishing returns. Opulent offices, for example, may disillusion a buyer by making a firm appear wasteful or unprofessional.

The process of identifying buyer purchase criteria should result in a ranking and sorting of purchase criteria such as that in Figure 4–4, which illustrates purchase criteria for a chocolate confection product. Price should be included in the list corresponding to the ranking the buyer places on it. Use and signaling criteria that derive from the end user and the channel should be separated, to highlight the different entities involved and to clarify the actions required to meet each criterion.

	Use Criteria	**Signaling Criteria**
End User	Taste Nutritional Value Texture Appearance Price Availability Package Sizes	Advertising Shelf Positioning In-Store Displays Availability
Channels	Speed of Order Processing Channel Margin Reliability of Service Promotional Support	Frequency of Sales Calls

Figure 4–4. Ranked Buyer Purchase Criteria for a Chocolate Confection

MEASURE OF VALUE

	Readily Measurable	Difficult to Measure
Lower Buyer Cost		
Raise Buyer Performance		

SOURCE OF VALUE

Figure 4–5. The Relationship Between Use Criteria and Buyer Value

Use criteria for both end users and channels can be usefully divided into those factors that lower buyer cost and those that raise buyer performance. While meeting a use criterion can sometimes both lower cost and raise performance, often one or the other modes of value creation is predominant—in the chocolate confection example taste relates to buyer performance while availability is predominantly a measure of buyer shopping cost. Then use criteria can be further divided into those that are easy to measure and those that are difficult for the buyer to perceive and/or quantify (see Figure 4–5.)

Recognizing the differences in use criteria represented in Figure 4–5 can be important for a number of reasons. Differentiation that lowers buyer cost provides a more persuasive justification for paying a sustained price premium with some buyers than differentiation raises performance. Financial pressures on buyers (such as in a downturn) often mean that buyers are willing to pay a premium only to firms that can demonstrate persuasively that they lower buyers' cost. Differentiation with a readily measurable connection to buyer value is also frequently more translatable into a price premium than differentiation that creates value in ways that are hard to perceive or measure. Differentiation that is difficult to measure tends to translate into a price premium primarily in situations where the buyer perceives a great deal to be at stake, such as in top level consulting or where the buyer is seeking to meet status needs. Differentiation on the right hand side of Figure 4–5 tends to be expensive to explain, requiring high levels of investment in signaling. Increasing buyer sophistication tends to threaten difficult-to-measure forms of differentiation that may have been accepted at face value in the past.

Each individual buyer to which an industry sells may have a different set of use and signaling criteria or may rank among them differently. Clustering of buyers into groups based on similarities in their purchase criteria is one basis of *buyer segments.*

Making Value Obvious for "Me too" Products

As I previously mentioned, when a product becomes a success, "me too" products show up; products copied from a successful business competitor. So, what should a product manager do if she or he has a "me too" product? How can the product manager make the value obvious when the "me too" product does not create a competitive advantage for buyers over the competition? The best way a product manager can make the value obvious for "me too" products is to leverage all the competitive advantages the company creates for its buyers by lowering the buyer's costs or raising the buyer's performance. Here is a list of some notable ones:

- Superior Customer Support and Service
- Superior Professional Services
- Financing and Leasing Options
- Complementary Products or Solutions

- Strong Partnerships
- Awards
- Certifications

Every one of these can create competitive advantages for a product's buyers. If the competition does not have it or is not recognized for it and it is of value to the customer, the product manager should use it in the positioning of the product. For example, Layer 2 Ethernet switches are sold by more than twenty equipment providers, and have relatively the same functionality. Accordingly, a product manager for a Layer 2 Ethernet switch that does not create competitive advantages over the competition should leverage all the competitive advantages her or his company creates for its buyers that lowers the buyer's costs or raises the buyer's performance. Doing it this way strengthens the value of the "me too" product, since the product alone does not create competitive advantages for its buyers over the competition. What's more, the value will be obvious to buyers, making them more willing to buy the product at a premium price.

Superior Customer Support and Service and "Me Too" Products

Data centers and networks play a mission critical role within every vertical market including education, financial, government, healthcare, manufacturing, retail, transportation, and so on. In most cases, data centers and networks are tied directly to the bottom line of a corporation, institution, or government; therefore, superior customer support and service can add value to a "me too" product. For example, in 1999, WorldCom's Frame Relay data service experienced a network outage that caused a large financial institution to lose over thirty three billion dollars in one day. Another financial institution lost over three hundred billion dollars. Both of these financial institutions were a customer of mine. What is obvious is that the impact from the network outage was significantly costly for both of these financial institutions as well as other institutions, corporations, and government entities throughout the United States. If the company of a product manager for a "me too" product offers superior customer support and service, the product manager should use the company's status in offering superior customer support and service in the positioning of his or her product. It will let buyers know that they are purchasing a product from a company that offers superior customer support and service, which will lower the buyer's costs or raise the buyer's performance. Given the mission critical nature of data centers and networks for corporations, institutions, and government entities, knowing a company offers superior customer support and service would be of significant value to buyers and make them more willing to purchase a "me too" product at a premium price.

Superior Professional Services and "Me Too" Products

When a high-tech company offers professional services to buyers of its products, it enables the buyer to get the most value out of the company's products, so offering professional services can add value to a "me too" product. For example, I once worked at a storage company on the creation of a business requirements document for an internal pricing web portal to support the worldwide sales organization. After creating the business requirements document, it was submitted to the I.T. department to be implemented; however, when the I.T. department responded back they informed me it would be eighteen months *before* they could start the project. Clearly, this company was in need of superior professional services since the backlog of projects had become so large it prevented the I.T. department from adequately providing timely customer support and service to the internal departments in the company. How well a company executes will determine its success. Buyers that purchase superior professional services can greatly improve the execution of their company. For this reason, if a company offers superior professional services, the product manager of a "me too" product should communicate the service offering in the positioning of his or her product. Buyers will want to know they are purchasing a product from a company that offers superior professional services since it can lower the buyer's cost or raise the buyer's performance. An I.T. department is only as valuable as the service it provides to the internal departments in the company, so purchasing a product from a company that offers superior professional services would be considerably valuable to buyers, making them less reluctant to purchase a "me too" product at a premium price.

Finance and Leasing Options and "Me Too" Products

As I mentioned previously, the economic downturn in 2008 caused many companies to significantly reduce spending, reprioritize projects, and create new business models in order to survive. Since in most cases high-tech products are large purchases and buyers consider them an investment, if a company offers finance and leasing options it can add value to a "me too" product. As a result, if finance and leasing options are offered by the company of a product manager for a "me too" product, he or she should communicate the finance and leasing options in the positioning of his or her product. Buyers certainly will want to know if finance and leasing options are available because it can lower the buyer's costs or raise the buyer's performance. Finance and leasing options can provide significant benefits to buyers, especially during an economic downturn such as preserve cash and credit lines, spread the total cost over a period of time, and keep their data centers and networks current with the newest technology while minimizing the risk of obsolescence. Thus, knowing a company offers financing and leasing options would be of significant value to buyers and make them more willing to purchase a "me too" product at a premium price.

Complementary Products or Solutions and "Me Too" Products

As I mentioned in Chapter 1, when a product does not provide a complete solution it can force the buyer to spend more time and money than anticipated to create the complete solution, so offering complementary products through partnerships or developing complementary products in-house can add value to a "me too" product. For example, during the time when I held the role as the product manager for the integrated router card the innovations of voice over packet networks had emerged in the high-tech market. Specifically, voice over frame relay (VoFR) and voice over IP (VoIP) access devices had emerged as a low cost alternative voice solution to voice over the PSTN; moreover, they were extremely attractive for service providers and enterprises in developing nations across Eastern Europe and Asia where PSTN infrastructures were quite sparse. As a result, by partnering with the companies offering the voice over IP (VoIP) and voice over frame relay (VoFR) network access devices, I was able to provide a complete solution for voice and data over packet networks to my buyers in these regions of the world. Therefore, if the product manager for a "me too" product can offer complementary products, he or she should include the complementary products in the positioning of the "me too" product and articulate how the products complement each other. Buyers will appreciate knowing they can purchase a complete solution from the company since it will lower the buyer's costs or raise the buyer's performance. Offering complementary products can reduce hidden costs associated with the purchase of a high-tech product; so knowing a company offers complementary products would be of tremendous value to buyers and make them more willing to purchase a "me too" product at a premium price.

Awards and "Me Too" Products

Every year industry associations and publications recognize top performers in the high-tech industry. As a result, if a company becomes the recipient of an award, it can add value to a "me too" product. For example, Cisco sells both innovative and "me too" products—it is well known in the industry that Cisco takes pride in their products being number one or number two in market share. Thus, if a product cannot achieve number one or number two status, they have been known to leave the business. What is more, as I wrote in my introduction, Cisco has always sold its products at a premium price for both their innovative and "me too" products. In addition, Cisco has been decorated with many awards for excellence in customer service. In fact, in both 2011 and 2012, Cisco was awarded the Technology Services Industry Association (TSIA) STAR Award for excellence in online support and service delivery optimization. It is one of the highest honors in the technology services industry. Furthermore, since the STAR award is only given to one company in every category every year, the award allows Cisco to be uniquely able to create competitive advantage for its buyers by lowering the buyer's cost or raising the buyer's performance. For this reason, every Cisco product manager of a "me too" product should have this award in the positioning of her or his product. It will let buyers know that they are purchasing a product from a company awarded for superior customer support and service, which will lower the buyer's costs or raise the buyer's performance. Of course, knowing Cisco had been given the STAR award would naturally be of value to buyers and make them more willing to buy a "me too" product at a premium price.

Strong Partnerships and "Me Too" Products

Strong partnerships are one of the best ways to add value to a "me too" product, since partners can leverage a product manager's product in selling their solutions. For example, an account manager submits an RFP (request for proposal) for a very large network opportunity from a retail chain that has three large data centers and over 1200 stores. The bid is for a solution to connect all the stores to the three data centers that included multiple types of networking equipment such as routers, channel extension devices, and network transport equipment. As a result, two months after submitting the proposal the account manager, his sales support consultant, and the other finalists are invited to meet with the retail chain to respond to further inquiries. However, at the meeting everyone in the room is a network equipment vendor with the exception of two individuals who represented service providers that have partnerships with network equipment vendors. Whatever happens amongst the entire group of finalist for the bid, the service providers are uniquely able to create competitive advantage for the buyer that the other finalist could not by offering communication lines and the network equipment. In fact, they completely changed the game. The bid was no longer about the networking equipment; it was about the communication lines that connected the data centers to the stores.

Partnerships can be very powerful. In this example, the service providers' real interest was not in selling the network equipment. Their interest was in selling communication lines and their partnerships with network equipment vendors provided them with the means to get in front of the retail chain and sell the communication lines, which would lower the buyer's costs or raise the buyer's performance. Most importantly, the service providers created competitive advantages for the buyer that none of the network equipment vendors could put on the table, the communication lines, which gave them the competitive advantage over the network equipment vendors.

If the product manager's company has strong partnerships, there will be opportunities where he or she can create competitive advantages in lowering the buyer's costs or raising the buyer's performance that the competition cannot. When an opportunity shows up where the partner's value can be leverage, the partner can have a huge impact on securing the deal. Partners can be the game changer in conducting business with buyers; moreover, since a partner has many loyal customers, a far reach, and a strong brand, there is an added value for buyers in being able to purchase the product from a company who they trust, making them more willing to purchase a "me too" product at a premium price. Thus, product managers of a "me too" product should acknowledge their partnerships in the positioning of the product to make the value obvious to their buyers. When the value is obvious, the buyer is less reluctant to pay a premium price.

Certifications and "Me Too" Products

Data centers and networks are mission critical and tied directly to the bottom line of any business, institution, or government. As a result, if a high-tech company offers certification training on its products and solutions, it will add value to a "me too" product. Buyers want to know the technical support and service they receive from their employees and the seller's employees will be of the highest quality since a network or datacenter outage will be extremely costly to their company. If certification training is available for a "me too" product or solution, the product manager should articulate the certification training in the positioning of his or her product. The product manager should also provide directions for buyers on how to locate certified channel partners, distributors, and resellers. Doing it this way will let buyers know that they are purchasing a product from a company that offers the highest levels of technical support and service, which will lower the buyer's costs or raise the buyer's performance. High-tech companies that offer certification training minimize the risks associated with the purchase of their products and solutions, including lowering the costs of downtime. For this reason, knowing a company offers certification training that results in a higher quality of technical support and service would be considerably valuable to buyers, making them less reluctant to purchase a "me too" product at a premium price.

To summarize, product managers of "me too" products need to leverage how their company creates competitive advantages for its buyers. It does not have to be one of the notable competitive advantages listed above. Maybe the company has a strong distribution channel that can get product to customers more quickly, which creates a competitive advantage for their buyers by lowering the buyer's costs or raising the buyer's performance. Accordingly, the product manager must get familiar with how their company creates competitive advantages for its buyers. Then, the product manager must make the value obvious to their customers so they will be less reluctant to pay a premium price.

Michael Porter on The Cost of Differentiation[10]

Differentiation is usually costly. A firm must often incur costs to be unique because uniqueness requires that it perform value activities better than competitors. Providing superior applications engineering support usually requires additional engineers, for example, while a highly skilled sales force typically costs more than a less skilled one. Achieving greater product durability than competitors may well require more material content or more expensive materials—Rockwell's water meters are more durable than competitors' because they employ more bronze.

Some forms of differentiation are clearly more costly than others. Differentiation that results from superior coordination of linked value activities may not add much cost, for example, nor may better product performance that results from closer parts tolerances achieved through an automated machining center. In diesel locomotives, the higher tolerances achieved through auto-mation improve fuel efficiency at low additional cost. Similarly, differentiating through having more product features is likely to be more costly than differentiating through having different but more desired features.

The cost of differentiation reflects the *cost drivers* of the value activities on which uniqueness is based. The relationship between uniqueness and cost drivers takes two related forms:

- what makes an activity unique (uniqueness drivers) can impact cost drivers
- the cost drivers can affect the cost of being unique

In pursuing differentiation, a firm often affects the cost drivers of an activity adversely and deliberately adds cost. Moving an activity close to the buyer, for example, may raise cost because of the effect of the location cost driver. Smith International achieved differentiation in drill bits by maintaining large and more accessible inventories in the field, raising its cost.

At the same time as uniqueness often raises cost by affecting the cost drivers, the cost drivers determine how costly differentiation will be. A firm's position vis-à-vis cost drivers will determine how costly a particular differentiation strategy will be relative to competitors. The cost of providing the most sales force coverage, for example, will be affected by whether there are economies of scale in the operation of the sales force. If economies of scale exist they may reduce the cost of increased coverage and make such coverage less costly for a firm with a large local market share.

Scale interrelationships, learning, and timing are particularly important cost drivers in affecting the cost of differentiation. Though scale can itself lead to differentiation, it most often affects the cost of differentiation. Scale can determine the cost of a firm's policy choice to advertise heavily, for example, or the cost of rapid introduction of new models. Sharing also can reduce the cost of differentiation. IBM's highly trained, experienced sales force is made less expensive by sharing it among a variety of related office products, for example. A firm moving faster down the learning curve in a differentiating activity will gain a cost advantage in differentiating, while moving early may lower the cost of differentiating in areas such as advertising where there is an accumulating stock of goodwill or other intangible assets.

The cost drivers thus play an important role in determining the success of differentiation strategies and have important competitive implications. If competitors have different relative positions vis-à-vis important cost drivers, their cost of achieving uniqueness in the affected activity will differ. Similarly, different forms of differentiation are relatively more or less costly for a firm depending on its situation vis-à-vis the cost drivers of the affected activities. Manufacturing parts with higher precision through automation can be less costly for a firm that can share the computerized machining center via interrelationships than for a firm that cannot. Similarly, Black & Decker has a faster rate of new product introduction than competitors in power tools but this rate is proportionally less costly for Black & Decker because of its leading worldwide market share. In the extreme, a firm may have such a large cost advantage in differentiating a particular value activity that its cost in that activity is actually lower than a firm not attempting to be unique in the activity. This is one reason why a firm can sometimes be both low cost and differentiated simultaneously.

Sometimes making an activity unique also simultaneously lowers cost. For example, integration may make an activity unique but also lower cost if integration is a cost driver. Where achieving differentiation and reducing cost can take place simultaneously, however, this suggests that (1) a firm *has not been fully exploiting all the opportunities to lower cost*; (2) being unique in an activity was formerly judged undesirable; or (3) a significant innovation has occurred which competitors have not adopted, such as a new automated process that both lowers cost and improves quality.

Firms often fail to exploit opportunities to lower cost through coordination of linked activities that also raises differentiation. Better coordination of quotations, procurement, and manufacturing scheduling may lower inventory cost at the same time as it shortens delivery lead time, for example. More extensive inspection by suppliers may lower a firm's inspection cost at the same time that the reliability of the end product is increased. Unexploited opportunities to reduce cost through linkages that also affect quality, in fact, are the reason underpinning the popular assertion that "quality is free." The possibility of simultaneously raising differentiation and reducing cost through linkages exists, however, because the firm has not been fully exploiting cost reduction opportunities and not because differentiation is not costly.

If a firm has been aggressively reducing its cost, therefore attempts to achieve uniqueness usually raise cost. Similarly, once competitors imitate a major innovation a firm can remain differentiated only by adding cost. In assessing the cost of differentiation, then, a firm must compare the cost of being unique in an activity with the cost of being equal to competitors.

Making Value Obvious in the Pricing Strategy

The role of price is to represent the value in the positioning of a product, not the value based on the cost to produce the product. Too often, I have seen product managers treat pricing of a product as a simple exercise where they calculate the cost of producing the product and mark up the price to achieve a target product margin. Alternatively, I have seen a lot of product managers spend countless hours devising ways to compete based on price. These approaches will quickly diminish the value of a product.

The best approach is to find the competitive advantages the product creates for its buyer by conducting the real-world cost of ownership analysis. If the product can create competitive advantages for its buyers better than the competition in lowering the buyer's cost or raising the buyer's performance, the product manager should articulate the value in the positioning of the product and price the product at a premium to the competition. Likewise, if the product is a "me too" product, but the company creates competitive advantages for its buyers better the competition in lowering the buyer's cost or raising the buyer's performance, again the product manager should articulate the value in the positioning of the product and price the product at a premium to the competition. Of course, if neither of these scenarios exists, the product manager should focus on developing ways to create competitive advantages for their buyers that lower the buyer's cost or raise the buyer's performance, whether it is for the product or the company. The key to having a successful product is to have value that is obvious to the buyer—creating competitive advantages that lower the buyer's cost or raise the buyer's performance.

Another trap that prevents value from being obvious is when a pricing strategy does not reflect the buyer's requirement. For example, my first product the integrated router card only offered one software license that included all eight routed protocols. For years it had been sold that way, but after conducting market research and learning that the majority of buyers did not require all eight of the routed protocols, it laid the foundation for changing the packaging and the pricing strategy. Not only was the price wrong because of the lower than expected performance, the packaging of the product was unattractive for my buyers; however, once the packaging and pricing strategy were changed the value again became obvious to my buyers and sales of the integrated router card took off.

Making Value Obvious Isn't Difficult

So far in this chapter, I have established that making value obvious is a generally reliable practice for compelling buyers to be less reluctant to paying a premium price; moreover, making value obvious isn't difficult. It only requires finding the competitive advantage the product creates for its buyers that lower the buyer's cost or raise the buyer's performance. This can be accomplished by conducting a real-world cost of ownership analysis. In that exercise, the product manager should look for advantages that reduce costs, gain efficiency, maximize revenue, increase productivity, or reduce time to market. The key is to identify what value the product offers and translate the value into creating competitive advantage for buyers by lowering the buyer's cost or raising the buyer's performance.

For example, if solid-state drive (SSD) storage arrays enable the buyer to use less floor space and saves on energy costs, it translates into CAPEX and OPEX savings for the buyer; therefore, solid-state drive (SSD) storage arrays lowers the buyer's cost. On the other hand, if soft keys on a smartphone allow the product manager to offer a larger screen, it translates into a gain in operational efficiency for the buyer because it allows the buyer to do more with the smartphone such as play games, watch videos, read documents, and so on. Hence, a larger screen that uses soft keys on a smartphone raises the buyer's performance. Then again, if a service provider core-router provides a securities firm's trading floor with five nines (.99999) availability, the securities firm has a high probability of never experiencing network outages. This translates into extensive costs savings and higher profits in the execution of trades; and so, the service provider core-router lowers the buyer's cost and raises the buyer's performance.

Creating competitive advantages for buyers by lowering the buyer's cost or raising the buyer's performance allows the product manager to price the product based on the actual value it deserves. Making the value obvious in the positioning of the product helps the buyer see the actual value of the product. There is a whole lot of truth in the saying, "Seeing is believing." If the buyer can see the value, he or she will be less reluctant to purchase the product at the premium price, but the buyer has to see that the value lowers the buyer's cost or raises the buyer's performance.

Michael Porter on Buyer Perception of Value[11]

Whatever the value a firm provides its buyers; buyers often have a difficult time assessing it in advance. Even careful inspection and test driving a truck, for example, does not allow the buyer to assess completely its comfort, durability, fuel usage, and repair frequency. A detailed understanding of how the physical product affects a buyer's cost or performance often requires extensive experience in its use. A buyer faces an even more difficult challenge in knowing how all the other activities a firm performs will affect the buyer value. Moreover, a buyer cannot always completely or accurately gauge the performance of a firm and its product even *after* the product has been purchased and used.

Buyers, then, frequently do not fully understand all the ways in which a supplier actually or potentially might lower their costs or improve performance—that is, buyers often do not know what they *should* be looking for in a supplier. While buyers are more likely to understand the direct impacts of a firm on their value chains, they often fail to recognize the indirect impacts or the ways in which other supplier activities besides the product affect them. Buyers can sometimes perceive too much value just as they can fail to perceive enough. For example, buyers sometimes see only the price of a product when measuring its value and do not add up other, more hidden, costs such as freight or installation. The buyer's perception of a firm and its product, therefore, can be as important as the reality of what the firm offers in determining the effective level of differentiation achieved. Moreover, buyers' incomplete knowledge of what is valuable to them can become an opportunity for differentiation strategy, since a firm may be able to adopt a new form of differentiation preemptively and educate buyers to value it.

A buyer's incomplete knowledge implies that the differentiation actually achieved may well be based in part on the factors used by the buyer to *infer* or *judge* whether a firm will lower its cost or improve its performance to competitors (or is doing so currently). Buyers use such indications as advertising, reputation, packaging, the professionalism, appearance, and personality of supplier employees, the attractiveness of facilities, and information provided in sales presentations to infer the value a firm creates. I term such factors that buyers use to infer the value a firm creates *signals of value.*

Some signals of value require ongoing expenditure by a firm (e.g. packaging, advertising) while others reflect the stock of goodwill or reputation a firm has built up over time. Similarly, some signals of value are not directly controlled by the firm at all (e.g. word of mouth). Signaling may be necessary, in some industries, to expose hidden costs of a product on which the firm has an advantage over competitors as it is to expose unrecognized benefits. In some, if not many, industries, signals of value are as important as the actual value created in determining realized differentiation. This is particularly true where a firm's impact on buyer cost or performance is subjective, indirect, or hard to quantify, when many buyers are first-time buyers, buyers are unsophisticated, or repurchase is infrequent. Good examples would be legal services, cosmetics, and consulting. However, the need to signal value is present in virtually every industry.

Buyers will not pay for value that they do not perceive, no matter how real it may be. Thus, the price premium a firm commands will reflect both the value actually delivered to its buyer and the extent to which the buyer perceives this value. This is illustrated schematically in Figure 4–3. A firm that delivers only modest value, but signals it more effectively may actually command a higher price than a firm that delivers higher value but signals it poorly.

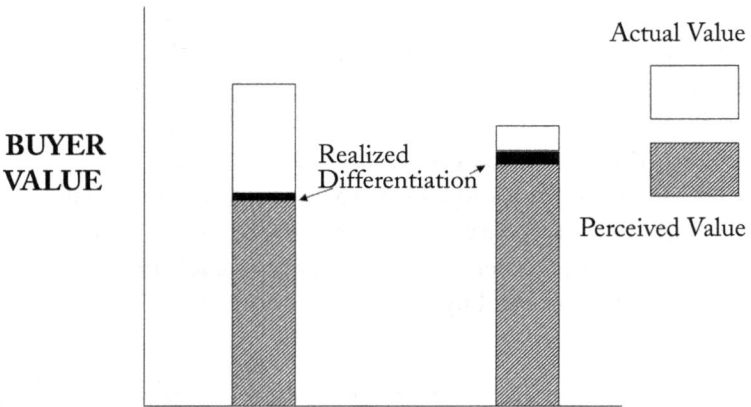

Figure 4–3. Actual versus Perceived Buyer Value

In the long run, the upper limit of the price premium a firm can command reflects its actual impact on buyer value—impact on buyer cost and performance relative to competitors. Through effective signaling of value, a firm may be able to command a price in excess of true value for a time. Eventually, however, the failure of a firm to deliver perceived value to match its price tends to become known, partly through the efforts of competitors. The converse is less true, however. By failing to signal its value effectively, a firm may never realize the price premium its actual value deserves.

3 | The Packaging Isn't Attractive

The packaging of a product is instrumental to the marketing strategy and the purchase of a product. As a topic of discussion, packaging is very broad since it covers everything from consumer goods to industrial, commercial, and institutional products. In any case, packaging is responsible for achieving several goals: establish the brand, communicate the features and benefits, promote and sell the product, differentiate the product from other products, and provide protection and safety for the product. Most importantly, the overall goal for the product manager is to make the packaging of his or her product attractive to its buyers.

High-tech products are industrial products; they are goods and services purchased for use in the production of other goods and services or used to conduct business. Additionally, high-tech products for the most part are customizable, so the purchase is more complex since it involves multiple components; therefore, how the product manager packages a high-tech product for its buyers can be a fortunate or regrettable experience. If the sales order process is too complex, it can change a buyer's decision to make the purchase.

For example, a company sells software to OEMs to reduce their time to market, but when the buyer orders a software license, there are many dependencies that required the purchase of additional software licenses as shown below:

1. Select the software license to order.
2. Does it require other software licenses?
3. Yes.
4. Select each of those software licenses.
5. Do they require other software licenses?
6. Yes.
7. Select each of those software licenses, and so on until all dependent software licenses required have been selected.

This is a cumbersome sales order process. It would frustrate any buyer; however, it could have been avoided if the product manager had bundled all the software licenses together so the customer would only have to make one selection. Unfortunately, this example is common in the high-tech industry for both hardware and software products. Typically, because high-tech products are customizable, a product manager will give every component a part number and let the buyer choose, but choice is overrated in the high-tech industry for many reasons. While sales representatives can ease the sales order process for buyers by walking them through the process, the piling on of too many choices can have a psychological effect on the buyer and diminish the value of the product whether the buyer is assisted or not. Too many choices create an exhaustive sales order process that will drive the buyer to expect a larger discount because it feels like more is needed than he or she anticipated was required. Hence, the buyer is no longer willing to pay a premium price. For example, I once worked for a network solutions company that sold five unique storage-management software applications separately. They had a large enterprise customer willing to purchase all of them under an enterprise license agreement, but only if they were sold together, like a bundle, using a single part number. The company accommodated them, but it just goes to show how sensitive customers can be about the packaging of a product when they make a purchase. One reason why a customer would make such a request would be to reduce the administration costs for managing the company's product and support contracts with sellers. In fact, I once worked for a telecommunications equipment company that had a service provider customer who placed them on purchase hold because they wanted to reduce the number of service and support contracts they held with the company. In other words, the service provider would not make any future purchases from the telecommunications equipment company until the number of support contracts between the firms was reduced to a manageable number, since the administration costs of managing its seller contracts had become a significant expense for the service provider. In any case, product managers who make their products attractive by streamlining the sales order process for their buyers will have a greater chance that the buyer will be less reluctant to pay a premium price.

To avoid unattractive packaging, the product manager should take into consideration the following when creating the packaging for the product:

1. The Complexity of the Packaging Strategy
2. The Attractiveness of the Packaging Strategy
3. The Clarity of the Packaging Strategy

The Complexity of the Packaging Strategy

As I mentioned in Chapter 1, when I was given responsibility for my first product, the integrated router card, it had been packaged with eighty-eight part numbers. Initially, I felt the eighty-eight part numbers was the least of my problems, since out of the six things I needed to address it had the least impact on bringing the product back to life. Specifically, I needed to repackage the software because of the lower than expected performance of the integrated router card, but as I was working on correcting that aspect of the packaging, I recalled the conversation with the account manager who told me it was difficult doing business with the company. As a result, I decided to change my focus to simplifying the sales order process. In fact, by making it my number one priority, it forced me to take a holistic view of the product and the buyers' requirements. It also forced me to understand that all six of the problems that were wrong with the product were relevant instead of just fixing the major ones. Specifically, both the loss momentum in the sales organization and the eighty-eight part numbers were equally relevant as the lower than expected performance of the integrated router card, the single software license that contributed to the lower performance, the number of routed protocols buyers typically use, and the current price. In any case, the eighty-eight part numbers were negatively affecting the buyer's purchasing experience with the integrated router card, which translated into diminishing the value of the product. As a result, I had to repackage the entire product to make the buyer less reluctant to pay a premium price.

It is not necessary to give buyers so many choices. They need to be led in the purchase of a customized product. They want to be told how they should buy. Who better to show them than the product manager? In my case, I was able to get the integrated router card down to thirty-five part numbers; twenty part numbers for the product and fifteen part numbers for the upgrades. The previous packaging of the product had a part number for every component in every scenario of every configuration of the integrated router card's hardware and software. Specifically, there were six hardware configurations of the router card and two I/O modules, so each I/O module was assigned a unique part number for each of the six hardware configurations. Technically though, there was no reason for each I/O module to have a unique part number for each of the six hardware configurations since it was the same card and they were sold separately. Consequently, the buyer had to choose from too many options. In the end, I was able to get the order process down to three components: a choice from two software packages available in four delivery methods, two hardware configurations, and two optional I/O modules.

By making the product packaging effortless, it streamlined the sales order process. What's more, because the new packaging was attractive, it added value to the product, which made the customer less reluctant to purchase the product at a premium price. In fact, the new packaging and pricing strategy resulted in an annual increase in revenue of 77 percent and 91 percent, sequentially.

My recommendation for creating part numbers is to be pragmatic. Keep it clean and simple. Too many choices will both overwhelm and exhaust buyers in the purchase process. Since going through this packaging exercise I have seen this problem with SKU creation far too many times. I have even named it as a symptom, SKU madness: a reckless act by the product manager who does not package the product to be attractive and easy for the buyer to purchase. A buyer's experience during the sales order process should never be ignored. A regrettable experience will diminish the value of the product, making the buyer more reluctant to pay a premium price. A fortunate experience makes the buyer willing to pay a premium price. A fortunate experience keeps the buyer coming back.

Another trap of SKU madness is the creation of part numbers for nonstandard transactions such as demo, evaluation, paid evaluation, and rental part numbers. This is completely unnecessary. There is absolutely no reason to assign part numbers for nonstandard transactions. Typically, the problem arises when a sales representative feels he or she needs a unique part number to enter a nonstandard deal into the customer relationship management system (CRM) such as Salesforce.com; however, because the relationship between a transaction and a part number is relational, all he or she needs to do is use the "Type" field in the CRM that describes the type of transaction for an opportunity, e.g., demo, eval, rental, new business, recurring business, etc. If the product manager accommodates these requests, eventually the product manager will have up to six times or more the number of part numbers needed, which clutters the company's business systems and makes reporting, forecasting, and strategic planning more difficult.

Another reason to avoid creating part numbers for nonstandard transactions is the psychological effect it can have on the buyer. Apparently, if the buyer wants to evaluate a product before purchasing it, the value of the product is not obvious yet, so why send an invoice with a nonstandard transaction part number on it. All it will do is to remind the buyer they have not made a purchase. Instead, give the buyer an invoice to purchase the product with a right to return over the agreed upon evaluation period. Doing it this way, the buyer will be more willing to buy the product at a premium price. It will also make it easier for the sales representative to close the deal.

Lastly, no matter if the part number is for product packaging or a nonstandard transaction every product manager needs to understand that there are costs associated with creating SKUs. Many people have to get involved to create a part number. Specifically, the manufacturing operations team has to create the BOM, put them into Agile, and have manufacturer SKUs created since most high-tech companies outsource their manufacturing. The I.T. department has to enter them into all the company's business systems. Finance will have to create the COGs and marketing has to put them in the product literature. What is more, customer support will have to create the corresponding support part number and technical publications will have to put them in the documentation. Therefore, if the product manager creates an abundance of part numbers because she or he did not think through the sales order process, it will cost the company a great deal of money in addition to creating a regrettable experience for the customer.

Here is my recommendation for creating part numbers. Spare manufacturing operations and everyone else the headache of dealing with SKU Madness by following this simple rule: create part numbers for product packaging with an emphasis on streamlining the sales order process. Do not create them for nonstandard transactions. It will reduce costs and makes for better reporting, forecasting, and strategic planning.

The Attractiveness of the Packaging Strategy

A packaging strategy should be strategic in making a product attractive. It needs to be ideal from the buyer's perspective. The attractiveness of the packaging strategy will determine the success of a product. For example, the single software license for the integrated router card was not an attractive packaging strategy. After conducting market research and receiving customer feedback, I learned that the majority of my customers only used the Internet Protocol (IP) and Novell IPX routed protocols, while a small minority of customers used more. Consequently, selling the software as a single license was not attractive to the majority of my customers. They were paying for more than they needed. As a result, to make the packaging attractive for my customers I offered two software license packages instead of one: a Base Routing package and a Global Routing package. The Base routing package included IP and IPX routed protocols, which the majority of my customers used, while the Global Routing package included all the routed protocols, which the minority of my customers used. By packaging the software to meet the needs of my customers, they were less reluctant to pay a premium price since the packaging better suited their needs. For this reason, it is important for product managers to understand their buyers' requirements. This can be accomplished through market research, surveys, focus groups, or through feedback from the sales organization or from buyers themselves.

Bundles and Product Line Extension

Two packaging strategies known for making products attractive is bundling and product line extension. Bundling is selling several products together as one product, while product line extension involves spinning off new products in the same product category. A good example where both strategies are used is Microsoft Office. On the one hand, Microsoft Office is a bundle of products sold together as one product. On the other, Microsoft Office is a product line that targets different lifestyles: Office 365 Home Premium, Office Home and Student, Office Home and Business, and Office Professional. By using both of the packaging strategies, the product manager is increasing the value of all the software products included in Microsoft Office. Buyers will appreciate the simplicity of purchasing all the Microsoft Office products together, while having the ability to choose the software package that meets their lifestyle. The packaging is attractive, which makes the customer more willing to purchase Microsoft Office at a premium price.

Michael Porter on Competitive Advantages of Bundling[12]

The potential competitive advantages grow broadly out of the ability to share activities in the value chains for providing parts of the bundle if the entire bundle is supplied together. The advantages of bundling can be grouped into a number of categories:

Economies of Providing the Bundle. A firm may lower its costs by providing only a single package instead of whatever mix of products or services a particular buyer desires. These economies arise from interrelationships in a firm's value chain that can be exploited by supplying only the package. Bundling can allow a firm to better share activities in the value chain in supplying the parts of the bundle. If the same bundle of products is sold to each buyer by the same salesperson, shipped on the same truck, or serviced by the same technician, for example, there may be cost savings in providing the bundle together. The price of the bundle could be lower than the collective price of the individual parts. For example, in providing services for offshore drilling for oil, a firm that provides two related services together may need only one person on the rig while competitors require a person for each service. Economies from bundling can also result from shared cost of gathering information about buyers. A consulting firm may learn about a client through providing one service, and apply this knowledge at low cost in providing other services in the bundle. The unbundled competitor must make the full investment in information even though it provides only one service.

Bundling may also reduce costs by promoting manufacturing economies of scale or learning. Providing the same package to all buyers guarantees an equivalent volume of all items in the bundle, perhaps lowering cost. For example, manufacturing a fire engine with standard features would allow a manufacturer to achieve greater economies of scale and learning than if each engine gets a different collection of bells and whistles, the current U.S. industry practice. Providing a common package may also increase the productivity of the sales force, by eliminating the need to inform the buyer about what parts of the bundle to select. Finally, bundling can significantly reduce administrative and selling costs. Providing the same package to all buyers usually simplifies transaction costs, including paperwork, logistical arrangements, and the like. Economies of standardization, scale, or learning can in some cases allow a firm to sell the bundle at a lower price than it would have to in order to charge customers who only wanted part of it. Economies from bundling will yield a substantial competitive advantage to a bundled firm only if unbundled competitors cannot duplicate them through coalitions or contractual arrangements among themselves. However, the difficulties of reaching agreement on such coordination with independent firms often preclude a contractual solution.

Increased Differentiation. Bundling may allow a firm to differentiate itself vis-à-vis competitors selling only parts of the bundle. The role of bundling in differentiation arises from linkages among parts of the bundle in the buyer's value chain because they are used or purchased together. Without bundling, a firm may not only forgo differentiation but be forced to compete with each specialist competitor in its area of greatest strength. Bundling can increase differentiation in the following ways:

More Bases for Differentiation. A firm that can bundle has more dimensions on which to differentiate itself than a competitor with a more limited offering. For example, a bundled firm may be able to guarantee reliability of the entire bundle or offer a single point for after-sale service. Similarly, it may differentiate itself or its service even though its product is not unique.

High-Performing Interface. Bundling may be necessary when the interface among complementary products is not standardized. Compatibility among items in the bundle is facilitated if the same firm provides the whole package of items needed jointly to meet the buyer's needs. This presumes that interface technology is relatively difficult, and that compatibility cannot be achieved.

Optimized Package Performance. Even if the interface among products in the bundle is standard, the bundled firm may be able to optimize the performance of the whole package (system) by controlling the design, manufacture, and service of all the parts. It may have better information about the capabilities of each part of the bundle than a specialist competitor who must gather information externally about parts of the bundle and cannot control their design directly. This advantage of bundling presumes that the parts of the bundle are interdependent in determining its overall performance.

One-Stop Shopping. Bundling simplifies the buyer's shopping task. Offering the bundle may also reassure the buyer that all the items in the bundle will work, and reduce the buyer's perceived risk of purchase. A single point of responsibility, a single place where complaints can be lodged, and a single service organization may also be valued by buyers. Buyer frustration over divided responsibility in the newly deregulated Bell System is a good example of how unbundling can lower differentiation through this mechanism.

Enhanced Opportunity for Price Discrimination. Bundling may allow a firm to increase total profits where different buyers have different price sensitivities for the individual parts of the bundle. Particularly in a "mixed" bundling strategy—where a firm offers both the full bundle at one price and the individual parts of the bundle at prices which sum to greater than the bundle price—bundling may increase total revenue compared to selling the parts separately.

The mechanism by which this occurs is a function of the cost of the bundle versus the cost of the parts of the bundle a buyer would want if they could be purchased separately. Bundling can cause some buyers to buy the whole bundle even though they would not buy all the parts individually, provided the incremental cost of the whole bundle over the cost of the parts they desire is low. In addition, a mixed bundling strategy can allow the firm to extract high prices from buyers who strongly desire only one part of the bundle, while at the same time selling the whole bundle to other buyers.

The value of bundling in pricing depends on the distribution of buyer needs in the industry. Bundling is most likely to raise profits if buyers have widely differing price sensitivities for parts of the bundle. Bundling is a way of capturing differing price sensitivities without charging different prices to different buyers for the same product.

Increased Entry/Mobility Barriers. Bundling may lead to higher entry/mobility barriers, presuming there are one or more of the other competitive advantages of bundling. Bundling raises barriers because a competitor must develop capabilities in all parts of the bundle rather than being able to specialize.

Mitigated Rivalry. Rivalry among a group of bundled competitors may be more stable than rivalry in an industry containing both bundle and unbundled competitors. If all competitors offer the same bundle and the only industry price is the bundle price, the ability to recognize mutual dependence among firms is likely to be higher and the incentives for price cutting may be less than if competitors offer any part of the bundle separately.

The Downside to Bundles and Product Line Extension

Alternatively, there are down sides to bundling and product line extension when not used properly that can diminish the value of the product. For example, a bundle should never be priced lower than the stand-alone price of any product in the bundle, which occurred at a network equipment company where I once worked. They sold a bundle for less than the stand-alone price of one of the I/O cards in the bundle, so buyers were compelled to purchase the bundle to get the I/O card for less. They would just throw away the other parts or put them in the grey market, which further diminishes the value of the product. In turn, product managers should adhere to this rule and never price a bundle lower than the stand-alone price of any product in the bundle.

Another common trap product managers make with bundling is discounting the total price of all the products to achieve the bundle price. This is not the correct approach to pricing a bundle. The better approach is to conduct a pricing strategy analysis treating the bundle as a single part number. This includes the product and gross margin analysis, the real-world cost of ownership analysis, and the packaging analysis. This will enable the product manager to test for healthy gross margins, identify the competitive advantages the bundle creates for its buyers by lowering the buyer's cost or raising the buyer's performance, and identify the best packaging strategy. Additionally, the product manager should leverage all the competitive advantages the company creates for its buyers by lowering the buyer's cost or raising the buyer's performance to increase the value for the bundle even more. My advice to product managers is to refrain from discounting off the total price when creating a bundle. It is the wrong message to send to the buyer and will diminish the value of the bundle. By conducting the pricing strategy analysis and making the value obvious to the buyer, they will be less reluctant to pay a premium price.

As I briefly discussed in Chapter 1, a common pitfall of product line extension is cannibalization by the lower extension product of the sales of the core product. I see this happen most when a product manager offers a core set of features for the lower extension product and both the core and advanced set of features for the core product. Typically, the idea behind offering a lower extension product is either to target a different market or respond to an attack by a low-end competitor. The difficulty arises when the lower extension product spills over into the core product's market and cannibalizes its sales. When this occurs, it is a clear indication that the value of the advanced set of features is not obvious to buyers.

One approach to handling a pitfall like this is to use an alternative packaging strategy. For example, the Microsoft Office product suite offers packages that target a different lifestyle: student, business, professional, and household, but the household package has an alternative packaging strategy to the other lifestyles. It is sold as a one year subscription for $99.99 and includes the entire Office suite plus cloud services for up to 5PCs/Macs and selected devices with ongoing version upgrades, all at a price less than Office Professional that is sold at $399.99 for one PC software license.[13]

In my opinion, this brilliant packaging strategy screams in value for Microsoft's buyers. Here is a list of the benefits I see. First, if a household has more than one PC/Mac, it is going to save them money. For example, if a household has three PCs and purchases a single license of Office Home and Student for each PC at $139.99, which is at the lowest end of the product line extension, it would cost them $419.97 instead of $99.99 for the annual subscription. Therefore, the household could purchase the annual subscription for 4 years and pay $20.01 less than the price for three Office Home and Student Licenses.

Second, although the subscription is only for one year, if the household purchases the subscription for four years, which is the average life of a PC/Mac, they will spend $399.96, which is almost equal in price to the single Office Professional license at $399.99. In other words, for three PC/Macs the household is paying the price of a single license for Office Professional. What is more, even if a household had only one PC/MAC, purchasing the annual subscription is a lot more convenient than purchasing a single license of Office Professional upfront.

Most importantly, the household would get the chance to experience all the advanced applications that are only in Office Professional; Microsoft Outlook, Publisher, and Access are not included in Office Home and Student. Consequently, instead of the lower extension product, Office Home and Student, spilling over into the higher extension product's market, Office Professional, this product manager created a situation where the higher extension product, Office Professional, spilled over into the lower extension product's market, Office Home and Student. This creates a competitive advantage for buyers since they will have access to all the applications in Office Professional, whereas, if the subscription were not available, they would be more reluctant to pay the premium price of $399.99 for Office Professional.

Lastly, the household gets an added bonus of 60 minutes of Skype calls per month to phones in 40+ countries and 20GB+ online storage with SkyDrive, which is more than triple the online storage of any other Office Suite. While these products are not part of the Microsoft Office Suite, it is a clever push strategy to get buyers to use other Microsoft products. Again, these bonus products spill over into the lower extension product's market, Office Home and Student, which creates a competitive advantage for the buyer.

Before implementing product line extension, it is important for the product manager to understand the risk. This is especially true for software products since the target market for advanced applications or features is smaller in most cases. No matter what, there is a high potential that a lower extension product will cannibalize the sales of the core product, but as the Microsoft Office example has shown, the product manager can prevent cannibalization from occurring by using an alternative pricing strategy to push the advanced applications onto the buyer through attractive packaging. The more common approach used by most companies is upselling where the buyer purchases at the low-end and the sales representative gets the buyer to upgrade to more advance features and capabilities over a period of time. Either way, there are downsides to product line extension that product managers should explore to prevent spillover into the markets of the other products in the product line.

Michael Porter on Bundled Versus Unbundled Strategies[14]

❝ The balance between the competitive advantages of bundling and its risks determines the appropriateness of the bundled strategy for a firm. The risks of bundling provide the strategic levers with which focused competitors attack bundled competitors. Bundling will be the predominant strategy in an industry if the competitive advantages of the bundled firm are significant and the risks of bundling low. Bundled and unbundled strategies are natural adversaries, however, and the balance between them can shift quickly in an industry in either direction.

In many industries, it may be difficult for the bundled and un-bundled strategies to coexist. If a successful unbundled competitor becomes established, this creates pressure on the bundled competitor to unbundle. The presence of an unbundled competitor makes buyers more aware that their needs are not being exactly met by the bundled firm, and provides an alternative to purchasing the whole bundle.

In entering an industry against bundled firms, an unbundled competitor is likely to attack those parts of the bundle that by themselves would fully satisfy the needs of a significant group of buyers, such as a basic product without the ancillary services. Another likely avenue of attack is to supply a peripheral item such as spare parts or service, where the bundled competitor is inefficient or overcharging. Attacking a bundled firm through unbundling is one of the characteristic ways of gaining market position.

After the first entry by an unbundler, the incentive is created for other unbundled competitors to enter and offer other parts of the bundle. Over time, then, more buyers are able to construct the particular bundle they desire. Once a number of unbundled competitors achieve significant market penetration, some of the motivations for bundling, such as scale economies, rivalry reduction, or building barriers, are often eliminated. Thus the remaining bundled competitors may be forced to unbundle.

The bundled and unbundled strategies can coexist in an industry, however, if there are wide differences in buyer needs and compelling advantages to bundling for some buyer segments that are *not* a function of volume (or of bundling being the dominant strategy). For example, optimization of system performance through bundling may be particularly critical for some buyers, and thus a bundled strategy will remain sustainable for this buyer segment despite the fact that specialist competitors supply parts of the bundle to other segments. Bundling may also be particularly valued by less sophisticated buyers, even though sophisticated buyers want to assemble the bundle themselves. In business aircraft, for example, Cessna is offering a bundle including a plane, maintenance, pilots, a hangar, office space, and landing fees all for a single monthly price. This appeals to buyers that want the convenience of one firm's taking responsibility for everything. A strategy of mixed bundling may also be appropriate depending on the particular competitive advantages sought from bundling. While offering the buyer an option to purchase either the whole bundle or parts of it from the same firm tends to undermine the firm's ability to sell the bundle, mixed bundling may be appropriate if the key advantage to bundling is differentiation or price discrimination.

The Clarity of the Packaging Strategy

The lack of clarity in the packaging strategy can be costly to a company. When a packaging strategy is unclear, it can produce unfavorable outcomes. Typically, this occurs in software licensing because the product manager is trying to control how the software is used. For example, a network solutions company sells storage management software based on the capacity of storage used by the buyer, e.g., the buyer has eight terabytes of data, so he or she would purchase a ten-terabyte license. On the other hand, the storage management software does not have electronic software licensing, which is a software license-management capability to prevent the buyer from exceeding the capacity that is licensed for use. Correspondingly, the company has placed the burden on the buyer to manage the use of the software. Typically, known as the honor system where the seller entrust the buyer to notify the company when they have exceeded the capacity purchased, so the license can be upgraded to support a higher capacity.

Unfortunately, this is a regrettable packaging strategy for several reasons. First, the packaging strategy is unpredictable and there is no guarantee that the buyer will honor the deal. I am not saying buyers are unethical, but when the product manager limits the use of the software based on capacity, it makes it easy to forget since the buyer cannot predict when an upgrade will be required. Buyers would constantly have to remind themselves to check the capacity every day. I doubt if any of them would want to do this. Even the sales representative for the buyer would have difficulty trying to keep up with predicting the timing for an upgrade. Second, even if the electronic software licensing had been implemented in the software, the product manager is taking a huge financial risk assuming buyers eventually will need to upgrade. The buyer has the choice to clean the storage continuously to avoid ever needing to upgrade. Third, the packaging strategy is inconvenient for the buyer since he or she would have to budget for the upgrade, even though it cannot be predicted when an upgrade would be required. Fourth, the packaging strategy is not attractive. The inability of not knowing when the upgrade will be required, and the inconvenience of not knowing when to budget for an upgrade diminishes the value of the storage management software, making the buyer more reluctant to pay a premium price. In any case, offering an annual subscription software license would have been a better packaging strategy for the storage management software since it would be more convenient for buyers in this example. The seller would have a record of the purchase date, so it could alert the sales representative ninety days in advance of the renewal or notify the buyers directly. No matter what, the packaging of software licensing should always be predictable and convenient. While the licensing should be very specific on use, product managers should avoid getting too fancy with it. There is nothing wrong with the honor system, but it has to be practical and not burden the buyer. Ambiguity will make the product unattractive and the buyer more reluctant to pay a premium price.

For these reasons, many product managers are turning to electronic software licensing that allows them to control the usage of their products; moreover, it can help drive revenue for their products in a predictable and convenient way without placing a burden on the buyer. The most common software licensing strategies are per user license, per installation license, per client license, per site license, floating license, open license, and royalty license. Each of these is easily controllable and is predictable and convenient.

To summarize, products in the high-tech industry are customizable, so the product manager needs to make the packaging attractive. Product managers can accomplish this by reducing the complexity of the packaging strategy, creating an attractive packaging strategy, and providing clarity in the packaging strategy. To reduce complexity, product managers should focus on streamlining the sales order process by making sure the product packaging does not overwhelm or exhaust the buyer during the purchase process. Most importantly, a product manager should avoid increasing the buyer's administration costs to manage their seller contracts. Doing it this way makes the customer less reluctant to purchase at a premium price. When creating part numbers product managers should be pragmatic. Keep it clean and simple. Too many options will overwhelm and frustrate buyers; moreover, there are costs associated with creating SKUs. Spare manufacturing operations and everyone else the headache of dealing with SKU Madness by following this simple rule: create part numbers for product packaging with an emphasis on streamlining the sales order process. Do not create them for nonstandard transactions.

Packaging strategies like bundling and product line extension can make products attractive. Customers will appreciate the simplicity of purchasing a bundle, especially when the packaging meets their specific need. On the other hand, watch out for the traps in bundling and product-line extension packaging strategies. Never price bundles lower than the stand-alone price of any product in the bundle. It will diminish the value of the stand-alone product. When product line extension cannibalizes another product's market, the product manager should look for alternative packaging strategies that will make the cannibalized product attractive to its target market. Instead of the lower extension product spilling over into other products in the product line's market, product managers should create situations where the higher extension products spill over into the lower extension product's market. This will increase revenue for the product line while creating competitive advantages for the buyer by lowering the buyer's cost or raising the buyer's performance.

The clarity in a software-license packaging strategy is instrumental to the success of the product. A software-license packaging strategy should always be predictable and convenient. There is nothing wrong with the honor system, but when it becomes a burden for the buyer, it will make the product unattractive, making the buyer more reluctant to purchase the product at a premium price.

4 | The Pricing Policy Isn't Working

Pricing is strategic to the success of a company. If policy does not exist to establish rules on pricing, it could have a tremendous impact on gross margins and the value of a company's products. At some point, every company will create a pricing policy. My recommendation is to do it as soon as possible. The role of the pricing policy is to establish rules and guidelines on anything that affects the price of a product. The most common areas addressed in a pricing policy are price lists, discounting, and sales promotions.

The Price List Policy

Price list policies focus on four key areas: price list creation, entitlement, uplifts, and foreign exchange settlement. The overall intent of the price list policy is to establish rules on how the company wants to conduct business with its buyers.

Price-List Creation Policy

The key objective for a price-list creation policy is to establish rules on how the company will go to market. In particular, a company must decide if they are going to create a single price-list for all their buyers or multiple price-lists for their buyers based on different routes to market such as global regions, specific countries, specific currencies, or distribution channels. Multiple price-lists are common for companies that do business globally or through distribution channels; therefore, policies for price-list creation will vary among companies depending on how they conduct business.

One benefit of having multiple price-lists based on global regions is that it allows companies to adjust prices to cover the cost of transporting a product from the manufacturing location to the buyer's place of business. This is known as geographical pricing, and the rules for establishing the adjustments are in the uplift policy. Uplift policies establish rules on embedding freight, customs, and duty charges into the price of products. Typically, decisions to embed uplifts is country specific and can vary as to which ones are applied; sometimes they are charged separately and not embedded.

Another benefit of having multiple price-lists based on global regions, especially in the hi-tech industry, is the flexibility it provides the product manager on where to sell the product. Sometimes this is necessary because of different technology standards. For example, digital telecommunications standards are different around the globe. The T-Carrier standards are in North America and Japan while the E-Carrier standards are in Europe and the rest of the world. To that end, if the first release of a product is designed only support T-Carrier standards, then the product manager has the flexibility to place the product on price lists only for countries that use the T-Carrier standards.

The benefit for having multiple price-lists for doing business through distribution channels is the ability it provides the product manager to control who can sell the product. For example, a company that sells products to both businesses and consumers has multiple routes to market. The business-to-business, B2B, products are sold through direct sales, channel partners, and distributors, while the consumer products are only sold through the company's online store and through retail distribution channels to retail stores. Accordingly, because the product managers for the consumer products only want buyers to purchase their products right off the shelf in retail stores or from the company's online store, they create a separate consumer products price-list for the online store and retail distribution channels. This prevents any confusion about who should be selling the consumer products.

Of course, the benefit of having multiple price-lists based on specific currencies is the ability to conduct business in the local currency of the buyer. I will discuss this more in the foreign exchange policy section coming up.

In any case, it is crucial to monitor processes that circumvent a price-list creation policy or it could be costly for a company. For example, a common practice I have seen in the high-tech industry is hiding SKUs on the price list. Typically, product managers will do this to limit who can sell the product to a buyer because selling the product requires special training. On the other hand, if a distributor were holding the product in stock during a stock rotation period, the operations team would not be able to validate the price of the product on the price list to process the stock rotation claims. As a result, the operations team may have no other choice than to allow the distributor to return 100% of the stock because they have no way to calculate the agreed upon percentage of product the distributor is allowed to return, making it costly for the seller. Moreover, because the product manager circumvented the price-list creation policy to hide the SKUs, which caused the operations team to allow the distributor to return a 100% of the stock, it could discourage the distributor from any desire to stock and sell the product in the future. No matter what, it is the product manager's responsibility to ensure that any time a nonstandard process is used in the selling of her or his product, such as hiding SKUs on the price list, that it does not affect the processes of other departments or teams such as sales operations.

Price List Entitlement Policy

The price-list entitlement policy establishes rules on how a company's buyers, channel partners, and distributors will do business with them. Specifically, the policy will outline rules for who is entitled to use a specific price list. For example, many global companies have a price list for different regions around the world, e.g., Americas, EMEA (Europe, Middle East, and Africa), and Asia Pacific. Hence, buyers in EMEA would be entitled to use the EMEA price list, but not the Americas and Asia Pacific price lists. On the other hand, if the buyer, channel partner, or distributor were a global company with locations all over the world, then the buyer, channel partner, or distributor would require entitlement to all the price lists applicable to countries where they conduct business.

A major objective in developing price-list entitlement policies is to prevent the occurrence of arbitrage. This is where an individual or group of individuals has discovered a way to buy a product in one market and sell it in another at a higher price. Rightly, it is beneficial to record the entitlement of price lists and audit them on a regular basis.

Buyer requests to purchase a product that is not sold in their country is a common problem that arises with the price-list entitlement policy; also known as cross border selling. Obviously, the product manager had a reason for not selling the product in the buyer's country. Unfortunately, a sales representative with such an opportunity usually will try to circumvent the price-list entitlement policy to make the purchase happen, which is not a good idea. Local support to install the product may not be available in the buyer's country, so the buyer will have to pay more for the installation because the seller will have to fly someone in from another country where the product is sold. Additionally, if local support were not available for installation, it would also not be available for on-site support, so again the buyer will have to pay more for on-site support. Moreover, if the product's documentation is not in the buyer's local language, they will not be able to read it. For these reasons, it is crucial for the product manager to enforce the price-list entitlement policy. The product manager needs to help the sales organization understand the impact of circumventing it. There is an old saying, "What seemed like a good idea at the time, turned out to be my worst nightmare." This is one of those ideas. Circumventing the price-list entitlement policy will diminish the value of the product, making the buyer more reluctant to pay a premium price.

Foreign Exchange Policy

Foreign exchange policies establish rules on the how a company will conduct business in different currencies. For example, if a company in the United States does business in Australia, the company needs to decide if they want to create a price list in Australian dollars or create the price list in U.S. dollars and adjust the prices to accommodate the difference in exchange rates. Some companies might do both. They will have an Australia price list in Australian dollars and a price list for conducting business in Australia in U.S. dollars.

Typically, the driving factor to conduct business in a different currency will be the volatility of the currency in conducting business. For example, a channel partner in the United States buys servers from a high-tech company in Germany and sells them to businesses in the United States. However, if the value of the euro changes dramatically between the day the channel partner orders the servers and the day the servers sell, the channel partner's profits could be lost in the currency conversion. Consequently, asking the channel partner to deal with the foreign exchange risk in the negotiation will make them more reluctant to pay a premium price.

Here is another example. A storage company in the U.S. sells storage arrays to businesses in Australia; however, the storage company will only conduct businesses in U.S. dollars to remove the need for any foreign currency swapping. On the other hand, if the value of the Australian dollar changes dramatically between the day the buyer orders the storage arrays and the day the buyer receives an invoice for the storage arrays, the buyer could end up paying more in the currency conversion. Rightly, because the storage company is asking its buyers to deal with the foreign-exchange negotiation, it will diminish the value of the storage arrays, making the Australian buyers more reluctant to pay a premium price. For this reason, product managers should meet with the finance department to understand how the company is handling foreign exchange risk to determine if the company's policy is affecting buyers' willingness to pay a premium price.

Another consideration in foreign exchange policies is the rules on adjusting price when there are fluctuations in the currency markets. For example, the global economic downturn in 2008 caused currency fluctuations all around the world as the price of gold and other precious metals rose because they were safer investments than currency. By and large, corporations will use a foreign exchange hedge such as a forward contract or option to eliminate foreign exchange risk; correspondingly, companies that don't use a foreign exchange hedge should establish guidelines on when and if an adjustment to prices should occur due to currency fluctuations.

Michael Porter on Segmentation Variables[15]

To segment an industry, each discrete product variety (and potential variety) in an industry should be identified and examined for structural or value chain differences from others. Product varieties can be used directly as segmentation variables. Buyer segments can be identified in a similar fashion, by examining all the buyers in the industry and probing for structural or value chain differences among them. Since buyers vary in a multiplicity of ways, experience has shown that a good starting point in identifying buyer segments is to look for buyer difference along three broad and observable dimensions: buyer type, buyer geographic location, and distribution channel employed. Buyer type encompasses such things as the buyer's size, industry, strategy, or demographics.

While these three dimensions of buyers are often related, each has an independent effect. Location can significantly affect purchasing behavior and the value chain required to serve a buyer even if all other buyer characteristics are equal. Similarly, in many industries the same buyer is reached through different channels; though the channel employed is often related to buyer type (and also to product variety). For example, buyers of electronic components purchase small, rush orders of chips from distributors and purchase larger orders directly from manufacturers.

To segment an industry, then, four observable classes of segmentation variables are used either individually or in combination to capture differences among producers and buyers. In any given industry, any or all of these variables can define strategically relevant segments:

- Product variety. The discrete product varieties that are, or could be, produced.
- Buyer type. The types of end buyers that purchase, or could purchase, the industry's products.
- Channel (immediate buyer). The alternative distribution channels employed or potentially employed to reach end buyers.
- Geographic buyer location. The geographic location of

buyers, defined by locality, region, country, or group of countries.

Identifying segmentation variables is perhaps the most creative part of segmenting an industry, because it involves conceiving of dimensions along which products and buyers differ that carry important structural or value chain implications. This requires a clear understanding of industry structure as well as the firm's and the buyer's value chain.

Product Segments

To identify product segments, all the physically distinct product types produced or potentially produced by an industry should be isolated, including ancillary services that could feasibly be offered separately from the product. Replacement parts are also a distinct product variety. Groups or bundles of products that can be sold together as a single package should also be identified as a product variety, in addition to the items currently sold separately. In the hospital management industry, for example, some firms sell a complete management package at a single price, while others sell individual services such as physician recruiting. The package should be viewed as a separate product variety for purposes of segmentation. Similarly, in industries where the product requires service, there are often three product varieties—the product sold separately, service sold separately, and the product and service sold together. In many industries, the list of product varieties that results from going through such a process is quite long.

Product varieties in an industry can differ in many ways that translate into structural or value chain differences and hence segments. Some of the most typical product differences that are good proxies for structural or value chain differences that define segments are as follows, along with some illustrative examples of why they reflect segments:

<u>Physical size</u>. Size is often a proxy for technological complexity or how a product is used, both of which affect the possibilities for differentiation. For example, different sized forklifts are typically used for different applications. Size may also imply differences in the value chain required to produce different varieties. Different sized varieties must often be manufactured on different machines, and require different components. For example, a miniature camera requires a different manufacturing process and higher precision components than a standard camera.

<u>Price level</u>. The price level of product varieties is often associated with buyer price sensitivity. Price also serves as a good proxy in some industries for the design and nature of manufacturing or selling value activities.

<u>Features</u>. Product varieties with different features may be associated with different levels of technological sophistication, different production processes, and different suppliers.

<u>Technology or design</u>. Differences in technology (e.g., analog versus digital watches) or design (front opening versus side opening valves) among product varieties can involve different levels of technological complexity, different product processes, and other factors.

<u>Inputs employed</u>. Sometimes product varieties differ significantly in their use of raw materials or other inputs (e.g., plastic versus metal parts). Such differences often have implications for the manufacturing process or supplier bargaining power.

<u>Packaging</u>. Varieties may differ in the way they are packaged and subsequently delivered, such as in bulk versus bagged sugar or draft versus canned beer. This translates into value chain differences in both the firm and buyers.

<u>Performance</u>. Performance differences such as pressure rating fuel economy, and accuracy are related to the technology and

design of product varieties, and often reflect differences in R&D, manufacturing sophistication, and testing.

New versus aftermarket or replacement. Replacement products often go through entirely different downstream value chains than identical new products, and may be different in other ways such as buyer price sensitivity, switching costs, and required delivery time.

Product versus ancillary services or equipment. The distinction between a product and ancillary products or services is often a key indicator of price sensitivity, differentiability, switching costs, and the value chain required to provide them.

Bundled versus unbundled. Selling various products as a package (bundle) versus selling individual items (unbundled) can have implications for mobility barriers, the ability to differentiate, and the value chain required.

The product differences that are most meaningful for industry segmentation are those that reflect the most important structural differences. There are often a number of different product descriptors that are related. Price level, technology, and performance may all be correlated, for example, and reflect the same basic differences among products. If each descriptor is measuring the same difference, the measure that most closely measures or proxies the structural or value chain differences should be chosen.

More than one product dimension may define relevant segments, and all product differences that affect structure should be identified. The best method for segmenting an industry in which there are multiple segmentation variables will be discussed below. It is also important in product segmentation to include product varieties that are feasible though not currently being produced, such as service sold independently of the product or a product variety with a new mix of features. Good examples are cordless telephones and the "no name" food items now sold in grocery stores.

Buyer Segments

To identify buyer segments, all the different types of end buyers to which an industry sells must be examined for important structural or value chain differences. In most industries, there are several ways in which buyers can be classified. In consumer goods, for example, some key factors include age, income, household size, and decision maker. In industrial, commercial, or institutional products, buyer size, technological sophistication, and nature of use for the product are among the factors that distinguish buyers.

There is an active debate among markets about the best means of segmenting buyers. In fact, no one variable can ever capture all the buyer differences that might determine segments, particularly since differences that affect the cost of serving buyers (and the value chain for doing so) are often just as important for segmentation as differences in their purchasing behavior. Buyer segmentation should reflect the underlying structural and value chain differences among buyers rather than any single classification scheme, because the goal of segmentation is to expose all these differences.

Industrial and Commercial Buyers

Common factors which serve as proxies for structural or value chain differences that distinguish buyer segments among industrial and commercial buyers are as follows, along with some illustrative examples of how they reflect segments:

Buyer Industry. The buyer's industry is often a proxy for how a product is used in the buyer's value chain and what fraction of total purchases it represents. For example, candy bar manufacturers buy and use chocolate much differently than dairy product firms, who use less chocolate and have less need for product quality. Differences such as these can affect factors such as buyer price sensitivity, susceptibility to substitution, and the cost of supplying the buyer.

Buyer's strategy (e.g., differentiation versus cost leadership). A buyer's competitive strategy is often an important indicator of how a product is used and of price sensitivity, among other things. Strategy shapes the buyer's value chain and the role a product plays in it. For example, a differentiated high-margin food processor is more concerned with ingredient quality and consistency than a private label food manufacturer that competes on costs.

Technological Sophistication. A buyer's technological sophistication can be an important indicator of its susceptibility to differentiation and resulting price sensitivity. Major oil companies tend to be more sophisticated buyers of oil field services and equipment than independent, for example.

OEM Versus USER. Original equipment manufacturers (OEMs) that incorporate a product into their product and sell it to other firms often have differing levels of price sensitivity and sophistication than firms that use the product themselves.

Vertical Integration. Whether a buyer is partially integrated into the product or into ancillary or related products (e.g., in-house service) can greatly affect the buyer's bargaining power and a firm's ability to differentiate itself.

Decision-Making Unit or Purchasing Process. The particular individuals involved in the decision-making process can have a major impact on the sophistication of the purchase decision, the desired product attributes, and price sensitivity. Many industrial products are purchased in complex processes involving many individuals and the procedures often vary markedly even among buyers in the same industry. Some users of electronic components purchase through trained and dedicated purchasing agents, for example, and are much more price-sensitive than other component buyers that employ engineers in purchasing or use purchasing agents also responsible for purchasing other items.

Size. A buyer's size can indicate its bargaining power, how it uses a product, the purchasing procedures employed, and the value chain with which it is best supplied. Sometimes *order size* is the relevant measure of size, while in other industries it may be *total annual purchases*. In still other cases *company size* may be the best determinant of bargaining power and purchasing procedure.

Ownership. The ownership structure of a buyer firm may have a major impact on its motivations. Private companies may value different product characteristics than public companies, for example, while a division of a diversified firm may be guided by purchasing practices determined by the parent.

Financial Strength. A buyer's profitability and financial resources can determine such things as its price sensitivity, need for credit, and frequency of purchase.

Order Pattern. Buyers can differ in their ordering pattern in ways that affect buyer bargaining power or the value chain required to supply them. Buyers that place regular and predictable orders, for example, may be much less costly to serve than those whose orders come at erratic intervals. Some buyers also typically have more seasonal or cyclical purchasing patterns than others, affecting a firm's pattern of capacity utilization.

Consumer Goods Buyers

Typical proxies of buyer differences that define segments among consumer goods buyers are as follows, along with illustrative examples of how they reflect segments:

Demographics. Buyer demographics can be a proxy for the desired product attributes, price sensitivity, and other use and signaling criteria. For example, single persons have different needs and purchasing patterns for frozen entrees than families with children. Many aspects of demographics can be important, including family size, income, health, religion, sex, nationality, occupation, age, presence of working females, social class, etc. In banking, for example, wealth, annual income, and the education level of household members all determine what banking services are purchased and how price sensitive the buyer is.

Psychographics or Lifestyle. Hard-to-measure factors such as lifestyle or self-image can be important discriminators of purchasing behavior among consumers. Jetsetters may value a product differently than equally wealthy conservatives, for example.

Language. Language also may define segments. In the record industry, for example, the Spanish speaking market worldwide is a relevant segment.

Decision Making Unit or Purchasing Process. The decision-making process within the household can be important to desired product attributes and price sensitivity. One spouse may be more interested in performance features of a car, for example, while the other opts for comfort and reliability.

Purchase Occasion. Purchase occasion refers to such things as whether a product is purchased as a gift or for the buyer's own use, and whether the product is to be part of a special event or used routinely. A buyer's use and signaling criteria are often very different depending on the occasion, even if the buyer is the same person and the product is similar. Purchasers of pens for gifts, for example, will favor recognized brands names such as Cross that may carry less weight in purchasing for personal use.

Several buyer dimensions may be important in defining buyer segments. In oil field equipment, for example, buyer size, technological sophistication, and ownership are all relevant variables. In frozen entrees, household size, age of family members, whether both parents are working, and income are all relevant variables. *Potential* buyers of a product not currently purchasing may also constitute segments. Buyer segmentation variables may also be related and the task is to select the variables that best reflect structural and value chain differences.

Channel Segments

To identify segments based on channels, all existing and feasible channels through which a product can or does reach buyers should be identified. The channel employed usually has implications for how a firm configures its value chain and the vertical linkages that are present. The channel can also reflect factors which are important cost drivers such as order size, shipment size, and lead time. Large orders of electronic components are sold direct, for example, while small orders are sold through distributors (often to the same buyers). Channels can also differ greatly in bargaining power. Mass merchandisers such as Sears and K-Mart have a great deal more power than independent department stores.

Typical differences in channels that define segments include:

<u>Direct versus distributors.</u> Selling direct removes the need to gain access to channels and may imply a very different value chain than selling through distributors.

<u>Direct mail versus retail (or wholesale)</u>. Direct mail eliminates the potential bargaining power of the intermediate channel. It also usually carries implications for value activities such as the logistical system.

<u>Distributors versus brokers</u>. Brokers typically do not hold inventory and may handle a different product line than distributors.

<u>Types of distributors or retailers</u>. Products may be sold through retailers or distributors of very different types, which carry different assortments and have different strategies and purchasing processes.

<u>Exclusive versus nonexclusive outlets</u>. Exclusivity may affect a channel's bargaining power and also the activities performed by the channel versus those performed by the firm.

There are often several types of channels in an industry. In copiers, for example, machines are sold direct as well as through copier distributors, office products distributors, and retailers. Channel segmentation must also include any potential channel that might be feasible. For example, L'eggs resegmented the hosiery market by discovering a new channel, the direct sale of hosiery to supermarkets.

Geographic Segments

Geographic location can affect both buyer needs and the costs of serving buyers. Geographic location may be important directly as a cost driver and may also affect the value chain required to reach the buyer. Geographic location also frequently serves as a proxy for desired product attributes due to differences in weather, customs, government regulation, and the like. For example, commercial roofs in the southern United States require less insulation than in the North, while the roofing membrane is more likely to be ballasted with gravel in North than in the South because a roof designed to take a snow load can handle the extra weight.

Typical geographic segments are based on variables such as the following:

Localities, regions or countries. Geographic areas may have differences in such areas as transportation systems and regulations. Geographic buyer location also plays a key role in defining scale economies. Depending on the geographic scope of scale economies, different sized geographic areas may be the relevant segments. In the residential roofing shingle industry, regions are the appropriate segments because high logistical costs limit the effective radius of a plant. In food distribution, metropolitan areas are the appropriate segments because of dense customer location and use of trucks for local delivery.

<u>Weather zones</u>. Climatic conditions often have a strong impact on product needs or on the value chain required to serve an area.

<u>Country stage of development or other country groupings</u>. Buyers located in developing countries may have different needs than those in developed countries. In addition, packaging, logistical systems, marketing systems, and many other aspects of the value chain may differ significantly. Similarly, other groupings of countries may expose similarities that define segments.

The relevant measure of geographic location for segmentation purposes will differ from industry to industry. In most cases, the relevant location to use in segmentation is the location where a product is actually *consumed* or used. However, sometimes the location to which a product is *shipped* (e.g., the warehouse) is more relevant. In other cases, the location of the buyer's *headquarters or primary dwelling* emerges as the most important geographic segmentation variable, even though the buyer uses the product somewhere else.

There can also be more than one meaningful geographic segmentation. For example, regions may be meaningful segments for determining cost position in industries where the costs of key value activities are driven by regional scale, whereas countries may be meaningful segments for determining desired product attributes and the ability to differentiate.

The Discounting Policy

Discounting policies establish rules for entitlement and nonstandard transactions such as volume purchase agreements. Generally, the deal desk that a company creates to handle the structuring of deals enforces discount policies. The overall intent of developing discounting policies is to protect the gross margins of products.

Discount Entitlement Policy

Discount entitlement policies establish the rules for discount limits for direct customers, channel partners, and distributors. Another intention for developing discount entitlement policies is to create fairness in transactions. For example, discount limits for channel partners typically are pre-established based on the partner's rank or grouping. Most companies use a tiered approach like Gold, Silver, and Bronze. The Gold partner gets the highest discount while the Bronze gets the lowest. The rank is determined by how much revenue the channel partner generates for the company, but some companies will rank their channel partners based on revenue targets as well as program certifications or specializations.

Appropriately, if a Bronze partner consistently gets approval for discounts at the Gold or Silver discount level, the product manager should consider it unfair to the Gold and Silver partners and in violation of the discounting policy. In my opinion, this is an egregious act when allowed to happen. The Gold and Silver partners worked hard to achieve their status, so the product manager should live up to the bargain made and enforce the discount policy.

What is more, the message the Bronze partner is sending the product manager is that the value of the product is not obvious to them or their prospects; correspondingly, the product manager needs to get to the root cause of the problem. Hopefully, the problem is that the partner needs training on selling the product; otherwise, the product manager should review the pricing and packaging strategies for the product to determine how to make the value obvious to the channel partner and their prospects.

The sales organization's hierarchy administers discount limits for direct paying buyers. For example, a sales representative has the authority to discount up to a certain limit. Any discount amount above that limit must get approval by a higher level in the chain of command or is directed to a deal desk for review and approval.

Accordingly, if the sales organization is consistently requesting larger discounts for a product, it is an indication that the value of the product is not obvious to the sales organization, which makes the buyer more reluctant to pay at a premium price. Again, the problem could be that the sales organization needs training on selling the product; otherwise, the product manager should review the pricing and packaging strategies for the product to determine how to make the value obvious to the sales organization and their prospects.

Distributors carry stock, so the discount entitlement policies are different for them. Distributors purchase products from a company at a wholesale price and sell them at the product's list price or at a discount off the product's list price to achieve their profit. There are times though when the distributor might ask the supplier company for a credit so they can sell the product at a higher discount. In any case, this should only happen with exceptionally large deals. If not, more than likely the distributor is selling the product as part of a solution with other complementary products, so the product manager needs to understand how their product is being valued in the solution created by the distributor. Specifically, the product manager needs to know if the product is being cross subsidized, sold at a low profit, by the distributor to sell complementary products for a higher profit. If found to be cross subsidized, the product manager needs to determine if there is a strategic benefit to allow the distributor to sell the product at a low profit. This scenario can also occur with channel partners and direct sales; however, while the use of complementary products would be obvious in a direct sale, the use of complementary products from other vendors would be less obvious with channel partners and distributors, so large discounts on smaller deals is clearly suspicious activity that deserves scrutiny.

Michael Porter on Cross Subsidization[16]

When a firm offers products that either are complementary in the strict sense of being used together or are purchased at the same time, pricing can potentially exploit the relatedness among them. The idea is to *deliberately* sell one product (which I term the base good) at a low profit or even a loss in order to sell more profitable items (which I term profitable goods).

The term "loss leadership" is commonly used to describe the application of this concept in retailing. Some products are priced at or below cost in order to attract bargain-conscious buyers to the store. The hope is that these buyers will purchase other more profitable merchandise during their visit. Loss leader pricing is also a way of establishing a low price image for the store.

The same pricing principle is at work in the so-called "razor and blade" strategy, which involves complementary products. The razor is sold at or near cost in order to promote future sales of profitable replacement blades. This same strategy is also common in amateur cameras, aircraft engines, and elevators. The complementary good is either a consumable item used with the product (e.g., film), a nonconsumable product used with the item (e.g., software cartridges with video games), and replacement parts (e.g., aircraft engine parts), or service (e.g., elevator maintenance and repair).

Another variation of cross-subsidization is a trade-up strategy. Here product varieties that are typically first purchases are sold at low prices, in the hopes that the buyer will later purchase other more profitable items in the line as trade-up occurs. This strategy is sometimes employed, for example, in light aircraft, motorcycles, copiers, and computers.

Conditions Favoring Cross Subsidization

The motivation for cross subsidization is clear—increase total profit by selling larger quantities of profitable goods as a result of discounting the base good. The logic of this strategy depends on the existence of a number of conditions:

<u>Sufficient Price Sensitivity in the Base Good</u>. Demand for the base good must be sufficiently sensitive to price that discounting increases volume (or foot traffic) enough to result in a more than compensating increase in profit through the induced sales of the profitable good. If demand for the base good is not sensitive to price, however, the firm is better off making normal profits on both the base good and profitable good.

<u>Sufficient Price Insensitivity in the Profitable Good</u>. The profitable good must have demand that is not very sensitive to price, so that raising price does not greatly lower volume. Unless this is the case, profits lost in discounting the base good will not be recouped through profitable goods. Insensitivity of demand to price in the profitable good is a function of the value it creates for the buyer and the threat for it.

<u>Strong Connection between the Profitable and Base Good</u>. The sale of profitable goods must also somehow be tied to the sale of the base good, so that buyers do not cherry-pick by purchasing only the low-priced base good. The connection between the products does not necessarily have to be binding, but it should be strong enough so that the proportion of buyers that purchase both from a firm is sufficient to justify discounting the base good.

The source of the connection between the base good and profitable good will vary from industry to industry. In retailing, the connection is created by shopping costs, which lead buyers to purchase other goods during the same visit to the store. In trade-up, brand loyalty and switching costs are the connection between one product and another. In a razor and blade strategy, brand loyalty and switching costs also may cause the buyer to purchase the blade from the firm that supplies the razor. In addition, perceived or actual compatibility may connect the goods (e.g., in film, spare parts), as does the belief of the buyer that the manufacturer of the product is best qualified to provide parts, maintenance, or repair (e.g., in elevators). The connection between the base and profitable good also depends on the possibility of substituting for the profitable good. If spare parts can be refurbished, for example, then there is no longer the same relationship between equipment sales and part sales.

Barriers to Entry into the Profitable Good. It must be difficult to enter the profitable good in order for cross subsidization to succeed, unless the base good and profitable good are strongly tied. Barriers to copying spare parts or consumables are essential, for example, to the logic of the razor and blade approach.

Risk of Cross Subsidization

The risks of cross subsidization tend to arise from failure to meet the third condition above. If the connection between the base good and profitable good is not sufficiently strong, a firm practicing cross subsidization may find itself selling only the low-priced base good and not the profitable good, which is purchased by the buyer from competitors. This can happen in a number of ways:

Buyer Cherry-picking. The buyer only purchases the base good and either does without the profitable good or purchases it from another supplier that is not cross subsidizing.

Substitutes for the Profitable Good. If the need for the profitable good can be eliminated or reduced, cross subsidization is compromised because the buyer will not purchase the profitable good. For example, refurbishing spare parts instead of buying new ones or increasing the life of consumable items would have this effect.

Buyer Vertical Integration. The buyer purchases the base good but integrates to produce the profitable good internally. For example, service is performed in-house, or the buyer fabricates or refurbishes its own spare parts.

Specialist (Focused) Competitors. A specialist competitor sells the profitable good at lower prices. For example, independent service companies are common in a number of industries which specialize in servicing a particular brand of equipment, or in copying spare parts. They target an industry leader, and perform relatively simple types of service or copy the most frequently replaced parts. The equipment manufacturer's margins on parts and service are thus undermined, and it may increasingly be left with only exotic repairs or low-volume parts. Sulzer Brothers, for example, is the prime target of unlicensed parts suppliers in marine diesel engines. The risk of entry by a specialist competitor is a function of the tightness of the connection between the base good and profitable good, and the barriers to entry into the profitable good. 　

Nonstandard Discount Policy

Discount policies for nonstandard transactions establish rules for deals with unique circumstances. The most common nonstandard discounts are requests for discounts that exceed the standard discount for a buyer, channel partner, or distributor. These requests normally are routed to the deal desk for approval. Another common nonstandard transaction is volume purchase agreements where the seller rewards the buyer for purchasing large quantities of the seller's product. Typically, the seller will create tiers for nonstandard discounts where a specific discount is tied to a number of units or amount of money spent over a period of time. Usually the time frame is based on the length of the contract; the most common time frame is a year. The tiered structure enables the seller to better manage the impact on gross margins. Like it or not, the seller must be firm on the discounts for each tier; otherwise, it is a violation of the discounting policy and will diminish the value of the product. Moreover, since these are volume purchases, an exception could severely hurt the gross margins of the product.

The Deal Desk

The deal desk provides direct support for the sales organization in structuring deals. Generally, companies establish a deal desk to improve the profit margins for the company. As a centralized function within a company, the deal desk addresses pricing, discounting, and other terms and conditions, but there are many other benefits in establishing a deal desk. A deal desk can improve the productivity of the sales organization. It can also enable a company to ensure Sarbanes Oxley compliance for revenue recognition. Moreover, a deal desk allows a company to create a central repository for contract creation, standardization, and resolution of contractual issues.

Typically, a deal desk analyst will coordinate the review process to ensure the deal is structured properly in compliance with corporate and government standards and policies. This may involve approvals from finance, legal, product management, sales, support, operations, and/or executive management. Often the deal desk will bring product managers into the structuring of nonstandard deals since he or she has the most knowledge on the product. No matter what, the product manager should review the deal desk activity for their product on a weekly, quarterly, and annual basis to understand nonstandard purchases of their products. The product manager should look for both positive and negative trends; any commonality in exceptions; consistent discount behavior by a sales representative, sales team, sales region, channel partner, or distributor; and anything else that could provide insight on ways to improve the sales order process, pricing strategy, or packaging strategy.

The Sales Promotion Policy

Sales promotions are short-term special offers or incentives directed at buyers, channel partners, and distributors. Product managers often use sales promotions to stimulate sales, attract buyers, or create market awareness for a product.

Sales promotion policies establish rules for promotions that directly affect the price of a product. Typically, price deals, trade-ins, and upgrade promotions fall into this category. The overall intent of sales promotion policies is to protect the value of the product.

Price deals are a temporary reduction in the price. Personally, I recommend avoiding them. There are just too many other creative ways to package a sales promotion. For example, instead of temporarily reducing the price, offer the buyer something they will benefit from, like a free training class or three months of advanced support. This gives the sales representative the opportunity to go back at a later date and upsell more training or an upgrade to advance support.

Trade-in and upgrade promotions are for getting current customers to purchase the newest version of a product. They also are used by the product manager to end-of-life older models of the product. Sometimes the trade-in or upgrade promotions are for an entire product while other times it can be for a certain functionality of a product, such as software or a new processor card.

The sales promotion policies for price deals, trade-ins, and upgrades establish rules on the duration, stacking of discounts, and budgets for sales promotions.

Duration of the Sales Promotion

The duration of a sales promotion can be costly to a company and diminish the value of a product. This is especially relevant when offering price deals that temporarily reduce price. If a sales promotion last too long, buyers will become more reluctant to pay a premium price in the future. Appropriately, the sales promotion policy establishes guidelines on the duration of the different types of promotions used by the company, e.g., price deals, trade-ins, upgrades.

In general, sales cycles for new prospects in the high-tech industry are long…often as long as six months to a year. Rightly, if the sales promotion is for new prospects, the product manager should take into consideration the average sales cycle for new prospects when determining the duration of a sales promotion. In any case, since the sales promotion is an incentive, it should never go beyond six months.

On the other hand, the sales cycle for an existing customer most often is shorter because a relationship already exists between the seller and the buyer. For example, the buyer has gone through the sales order process, is familiar with the seller's products, and has engaged with the technical support and service organization. Fittingly, a sales promotion targeting existing buyers such as a trade-in or upgrade promotion can be shorter in duration, such as one fiscal quarter or three months.

Then again, because the purchase of high-tech products in most cases will be large investments by the buyer, the product manager must take into consideration the timing of the sales promotion since the buyer may not have sufficient funds planned to participate. Accordingly, the product manager should announce the sales promotion to the sales organization including channel partners and distributors in advance of the launch to give them sufficient lead-time to notify buyers. Most importantly, the announcement should occur in the same fiscal quarter the launch of the sales promotion occurs. This is extremely necessary because announcing a sales promotion in a fiscal quarter prior to the launch will cause buyers to delay any purchases of the product until the sales promotion begins. As a result, the delay in purchases will negatively affect the company's revenue performance for any quarter prior to the sales promotion launch. For example, in the first quarter of the fiscal year, a product manager announces to the sales organization, including channel partners and distributors, a trade-in sales promotion for a new release of a line card in an optical network switch, but the launch for the trade-in sales promotion will not occur until the second quarter of the fiscal year. As a result, buyers withhold their purchases of the new release of the line card until the second quarter of the fiscal year; consequently, the company experiences a decline in its revenue performance in the first quarter of the fiscal year because of the delay by the buyers in making a purchase.

Stacking of Discounts

The sales promotion policy for the stacking of discounts establishes guidelines on when to allow a combination of discounts. In my opinion, the best guideline is not to allow stacking, but sometimes it is unavoidable. For example, buyers can combine the sales promotion discount for a price deal with a volume-purchase-agreement discount. As a result, the stacking of the discounts significantly affects the gross margins of a product since volume purchase agreement discounts in general are higher than standard discounts. It is for this reason I recommend avoiding price deals and offering a benefit instead. Trade-in and upgrade promotions will also fall into this trap.

One way to prevent default stacking from significantly affecting a product's gross margin is to limit the number each buyer can purchase under the sales promotion. Another alternative is to have the legal department put a clause in every volume purchase agreement that specifies that the stacking discount is not allowed, so the buyer would have to choose either their contractual discount or the sales promotion discount. Alternatively, the product manager can specify in the sales promotion not to allow other discounts. This may sound unfair, but allowing customers with volume purchase agreements to stack discounts can crush the gross margin of a product. Sure, the product manager wants its buyers to purchase the product and trade-in or upgrade to the newest version of the product, but since the company is already rewarding them for the high volume of purchases, it is not necessary to reward them again.

Sales Promotion Budget

Most companies allocate a budget for sales promotions to limit the amount of money spent. The reason for doing this is to protect the gross margin of the product. While it limits what the product manager can do, uncontrolled spending can have disastrous results. For example, an upgrade promotion runs too long, so the buyer is no longer willing to pay a premium price. Appropriately, the policy for sales promotion budgets is to establish guidelines on the amount of money that is allowed to be spent for each type of promotion used by the company, e.g., discount ranges and creating the budget as a percentage of total revenue forecast for price deals, trade-ins, and upgrades.

In any case, sales promotions require a lot of creativity; moreover, to make a sales promotion effective, the product manager needs to have the right information. Specifically, he or she should create a forecast on the quantity of products, trade-ins, or upgrades that will be sold over the promotion time-frame. For upgrade and trade-ins, the forecast can be easily determined by running a report of all customer purchases of the product, but I do not recommend forecasting every previous purchase since some buyers will not be ready to upgrade or trade-in at the time of the promotion. The overall objective is to determine how far the budget will go.

For example, a product manager wants to do an upgrade promotion for a processor card in a data center switch. Currently, he or she has sold one thousand processor cards. The list price of the new processor card is $35,000, so if the product manager offers a 25% discount that would equal $8,750.00 per processor card that goes against the budget. Multiplying $8,750.00 times one thousand equals $8,750,000 for the one thousand cards. That is the budget the product manager would need to run the sales promotion, but if the budget were only seven million dollars, then the product manager would have to lower the discount or reduce the forecast. Specifically, the forecast would have to be 800 units or the discount would have to be 20%. No matter what, if the product manager reduced the forecast to 800 units, the total revenue forecast for the sales promotion would be $21M. On the other hand, reducing the discount to 20% raises the forecast to $28M in revenue, so the more lucrative of the two strategies would be to lower the discount to 20%. Overall, the product manager could spend $7M to generate $28M in revenue that is four times the budget, which indicates a successful sales promotion. Alternatively, if the budget had not been in place, the product manager would have spent an additional $1.75M on the sales promotion.

To summarize, the role of the pricing policy is to establish rules and guidelines on anything that influences the price of a product. The most common areas addressed in a pricing policy are price lists, discounting, and sales promotions. The price list policy establishes rules on how the company wants to conduct business with its customers. The discounting policy establishes rules to protect the product's gross margin, and the sales promotion policy establishes rules to protect the value of the product. The product manager should stand firm on the pricing policy and discourage buyers, partners, and the sales organization from circumventing any of the pricing policies. Failure to do so will diminish the value of the product making the buyer more reluctant to pay a premium price.

5 Price Isn't in the Eye of the Customer

"Price is in the eye of the customer" is not as cliché as the fact that most people do not understand what it means. Price is in the eye of the customer means the total experience a buyer has with a company weighed against the price of the purchase the buyer made or makes over a period of time. Total experience means every interaction the buyer has with a company. From the sales process to ordering, delivery, installation, implementation, customer support, billing, trade show experience, and so on. Even a company's stock performance is part of the total experience the buyer weighs against the price of the purchase.

For example, if a buyer purchases $10 million in core-routers from a company and at least one core-router crashed every week. The buyer's total experience has been affected negatively and will diminish the value of the purchase. Furthermore, if the buyer contacts the technical assistance center of the company and cannot get timely help to resolve the weekly crashes, the lack of timely support will further negatively affect the total experience of the buyer with the company. Therefore, it is crucial for product managers to inspect every interaction a buyer will have with the company before, during, and after the purchase of their product.

Michael Porter on The Value Chain and Buyer Value[17]

A firm lowers buyer cost or raises buyer performance through the impact of its value chain on the buyer's value chain. A firm may affect the buyer's chain by simply providing an input to one buyer activity. Frequently, however, a firm's product will have both direct and indirect impacts on the buyer's chain that go beyond the activity in which the product is actually used. For example, weight is important in a typewriter that is moved from place to place though it is not relevant if one views the buyer activity simply as typing. Moreover, a firm typically impacts the buyer not only through its product but also through such activities as the logistical system, order entry system, sales force, and applications engineering group. Even firm activities representing a small fraction of total cost can have a substantial impact on differentiation. Sometimes the buyer has individual contact with value activities of the firm (e.g., the sales force) while in other cases the buyer only observes the outcome of a group of activities (e.g., the ultimate on-time or late delivery). Thus, the value a firm creates for its buyer is determined by the whole array of links between the firm's value chain and its buyer's value chain, represented schematically in Figure 4–2.

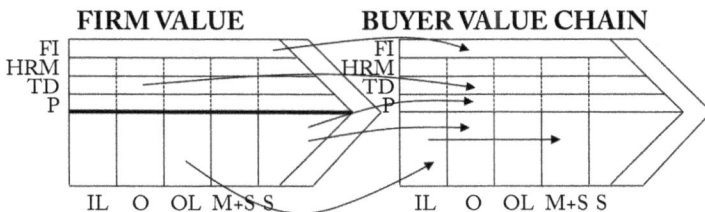

Figure 4–2. Representative Linkages Between the Firm and the Buyer's Value Chain

Heavy trucks offer a useful example of multiple links. A heavy truck directly influences its buyer's logistical costs—a function of the truck's carrying capacity, ease of loading and unloading, fuel costs, and maintenance costs. The truck will also have indirect effects on its buyer's other costs. Its capacity will influence the frequency with which the buyer makes deliveries. The truck may contribute product quality through the amount of shaking it subjects the cargo to, as well as the temperature and humidity conditions in transit. The truck may also affect the buyer's packaging costs, a function of the protection required to avoid damage. Finally, the truck may incrementally affect brand identity through its appearance and the visibility of the logo painted on the side.

Not only will the truck itself affect the buyer's value chain, but several other value activities of the truck manufacturer will probably affect the buyer as well. Spare parts availability will affect the downtime experience by the buyer. Credit policies will affect the financing cost of the truck. The quality of the truck manufacturer's sales force may well determine their helpfulness in suggesting new maintenance procedures and truck utilization practices. All these links between a truck manufacturer's value activities and the buyer may potentially add to or subtract from buyer cost or performance. The principle also holds true for household buyers.

The links between a firm and its buyer's value chain that are relevant to buyer value depend on how the firm's product is *actually* used by the buyer, not necessarily how it was intended to be used. Even the most carefully designed product can yield unsatisfactory performance if a buyer does not understand how to install, operate, or maintain it or if it is used for a purpose for which it was not intended. For example, a housewife may get terrible results from a frozen food product if it is cooked at the wrong temperature. Similarly, a machine can malfunction quickly if it is not oiled in the right place.

Every impact of a firm on its buyer's value chain, including every link between firm and buyer value activities, represents a possible opportunity for differentiation. The more direct and indirect impacts a product has on its buyer's value chain, the richer the possibilities for differentiation tend to be and the greater the overall level of achievable differentiation. A truck manufacturer with a sophisticated understanding of how it impacts its buyer's value chain, for example, can not only design the truck to provide greater benefits to the buyer, but can perform other value activities such as service, spare parts supply, and financing to be more valuable to the buyer.

Differentiation, then, grows out of all the links between a firm and its buyer in which the firm is unique. The value of being unique in a value activity is its direct and indirect impact on the buyer's cost or performance. A firm's overall level of differentiation is the cumulative value to the buyer of the uniqueness throughout its value chain. This cumulative value can be calculated and provides the upper limit of the price premium the firm can command relative to its competitors. Since the firm must necessarily *share some of the value* it creates with its buyer in order to give the buyer an incentive to purchase, the actual price premium will be somewhat less in practice.

While it would be difficult to achieve perfection across all interactions with a prospect or customer, since most often these interactions involve interfacing with a human being who the product manager has little control over, the creation of best practices for interacting with prospects and customers could reduce the number of unpleasant experiences they may encounter. Let's take a closer look at prospect and customer interactions.

Outside Sales Representatives

Outside sales is the primary contact for prospects and customers in the purchase of a company's products; accordingly, an outside sales representative must demonstrate professionalism, a friendly personality, excellent communication skills, knowledge of the prospect's and customer's challenges, and knowledge of the products he or she sells. Any disappointment experienced by the prospect or customer in her or his interaction with the sales representative will diminish their total experience with the company, making the prospect or customer more reluctant to pay a premium price. By this, I mean more than just a sales representative's lack of product knowledge or interest in the prospect's or customer's challenges. For example, if the sales representative arrives late for a scheduled meeting, does not return calls from the prospect or customer in a timely manner, wears unsuitable attire, or has poor hygiene will also negatively affect a prospect's or customer's total experience with the company. While a product manager has little control over the appearance and attentiveness of an outside sales representative, it is the product manager's responsibility to ensure that the outside sales organization has been trained on the features and benefits of the product. Moreover, the outside sales representative must be educated on the competitive advantages the product creates for the buyer. Most importantly, the competitive advantages the product creates for the buyer must be obvious to the sales organization so they can position the product to their prospects and customers in a way that will make them less reluctant to pay a premium price.

Empowering the Sales Organization

Product literature and sales tools empower the sales representative to communicate the features, benefits, and competitive advantages the product creates for their prospects and customer. There is though a broader set of knowledge the sales representative must possess to communicate effectively. One-approach product managers can use to provide this broader set of knowledge for the sales organization is to create a sales guide about their product that provides information on the following:

I. Product Overview
    a. The Market Opportunity
    b. Market Forecast
    c. Value Proposition
II. Target Markets
    a. General Target Market Segments
    b. Region-Specific Target Market Segments
III. Positioning into Target Markets
    a. Product Positioning
    b. Problem Statement
    c. Key Benefits
IV. Features
V. Standards Compliance
VI. Application Examples
VII. Competition
VIII. Pricing and Product Configuration

A sales guide is a valuable resource for focusing the sales organization in capitalizing on the right opportunities; appropriately, the product manager should update it at least once a quarter. Keeping the sales organization up to date on the status of the product is essential to the product's success. When out of date information passes on to prospects and customers, it will diminish the value of the product making them more reluctant to pay a premium price.

The product manager must also ensure that the sales organization has access to clear and well-written product literature such as data sheets, white papers, and application notes to enhance the sales process. Additionally, the sales organization must have access to professionally created sales tools such as slide presentations, webinars, video presentations, product demonstrations, and webcasts. Regardless of the delivery format, these sales tools must be well designed and not cluttered with too many graphics, animations, or text. The sales tools should be attractive to gain the viewer's attention and have a logical flow that compels the viewer to want to know more. They should highlight the speaking points of the presenter and not be too long.

In any case, poorly crafted product literature and sales tools will diminish a prospect's or customer's total experience with the company, making him or her more reluctant to pay a premium price. For example, long detailed slide and video presentations can overwhelm prospects and customers with too much information, while webinars and webcast that do not start on time and drop connections will irritate them. Accordingly, it is crucial for product managers to ensure that the product literature and sales tools create the best, overall experience for prospects and customers.

Packaging, Pricing, and Discounting

As I mentioned in the previous chapters, the packaging and pricing strategies will have a tremendous impact on a buyer's commitment to purchase the product. They too are part of the buyer's total experience with the company. Since products in the high-tech industry generally are customizable, it is crucial for the product manager to streamline the sales order process, which will simplify the buyer's experience in purchasing the product. This includes both the ease in ordering the product and the quote generation process. The packaging of a product is only as useful as the sales representative's ability to generate a quote. For this reason, the product manager should attend the sales training on quote generation to identify if there is any complexity to remove in the process.

Equally, since the goal of most pricing strategies is to achieve healthy gross margins, it is crucial for the product manager to acknowledge the competitive advantages their product creates for its buyers in the pricing of the product. As Michael Porter wrote, "Since the firm must necessarily share some of the value it creates with its buyer in order to give the buyer an incentive to purchase, the actual price premium will be somewhat less in practice."[18] Therefore, product managers should avoid pursuing a price advantage in the pricing strategy. Their focus should be on creating competitive advantages and making the value obvious for buyers.

Lastly, how the outside sales representative handles discounting will affect the buyer's total experience with the company. This is why it is crucial for the product manager to insist upholding the pricing and discounting policies. A company would do better implementing a profitability strategy than a revenue growth strategy, especially during an economic downturn because the profitability strategy will enable a company to preserve the value of its products. On the other hand, a revenue growth strategy will require heavy discounting and diminish the value of the company's products over the long term. Prospects and customers during an economic downturn have to reduce spending, reprioritize projects, and create new business models; there is no other choice, so a company would be wise to acknowledge the dilemma and put in place a pricing strategy that creates value for its products.

Outside Sales — System Engineers

Within a sales organization, there is a sales system engineering organization to support the sales representatives in the selling of products. The sales system engineering organization provides the technical support in the presales and often post sales process. Similar to the sales representative, the sales system engineer must demonstrate professionalism, a friendly personality, strong communication skills, technical knowledge of the prospect's challenges, and deep technical knowledge of the products he or she sells. Should a prospect or customer experience any disappointment in his or her interaction with a sales system engineer it will diminish the value of a product and the prospect's or customer's total experience with the company, making him or her more reluctant to pay a premium price. This also applies to the appearance and the attentiveness of a sales system engineer to the prospect or customer. No matter what, even though a product manager has little control over the appearance and attentiveness of a sales system engineer, it is the product manager's responsibility to ensure that the sales system engineers in the field have received the proper technical training since they engage with the technical employees of prospects and customers. For example, at times sales system engineers must give technical product presentations, product demonstrations, and/or provide on-site technical support to buyers when a problem arises.

Rightly, product managers should review and attend the product training for sales systems engineers to ensure the technical depth is sufficient for them to support the sales representative in the selling of their product. Attending will also allow the product manager to respond to any questions they may have about the product. In fact, often the product manager will present the product roadmap during sales systems engineering training to provide visibility into planned enhancements for the product. Knowledge about the product roadmap is instrumental to the success of the sales system engineer, since more often than not the purchase of high-tech products are sizable and considered an investment by prospects and customers. Buyers will want to be informed of future plans for the product; therefore, it is imperative for the product manager to ensure that sales systems engineers have knowledge about the product roadmap else it will diminish the value of the product and the buyer's total experience with the company, making them more reluctant to pay a premium price.

Product Expertise

Typically, the sales system engineer in a sales organization is considered the product expert from the prospect's or customer's perspective. In fact, for five years I held the role of a sales system engineer in the field, so I know how crucial it is for a sales system engineer to embrace the "expert" status in closing deals. A sales systems engineer must be able to instill confidence with a prospect or customer that the product will address his or her challenges to either lower cost or raise performance. Moreover, even though the sales system engineer in most cases interacts with employees who are not the decision maker for making the purchase, they are strong influencers on the purchase decision.

There are many unknowns about the prospect's or customer's premises, e.g. data center, so the sales systems engineer may not always have all the answers to a prospect's or customer's questions. Consequently, it becomes a balancing act of being perceived as the expert, but also being able to handle situations where further research would be required. Specifically, I have witnessed sales systems engineers who have handled these kinds of situations poorly by coming off cocky or becoming flustered in front of a prospect or customer; some have even lied to avoid the appearance of lacking expertise, which is not what he or she should do. Humility is always the best approach. For example, the best response when the sales system engineer does not have the answer should be, "That is a good question, unfortunately, I do not have the answer, but am willing to do the research and get back to you in a few days." Most importantly, the sales system engineer must follow up on the promise else, it will have a negative effect on the customer's total experience, making them more reluctant to pay a premium price.

Moreover, often companies will overlook the communication skills of sales system engineers in favor of their technical skill set. In a situation like this the company should provide training for the sales system engineer else the prospect's total experience could be diminished. If the company does not provide communication skills training, then the product manager should insist on training since improper or poor communication will have a negative effect on the prospect's or customer's total experience with the company.

Lastly, because high-tech products typically are customizable, it is essential that the sales system engineer understand the sales order process since their technical knowledge will be required to assist the sales representative in creating the purchase order for the buyer. Therefore, the product manager must ensure that training on the sales order process is available for sales system engineers. Typically, the sales system engineers can attend the sales order training conducted for sales representatives.

Inside Sales Representatives

Inside sales is the most valuable function in the follow-up from lead generation since they are the initial contact with a new prospect. The inside sales representative's professionalism, inviting personality, persuasive communication and phone skills, excellent listening skills, knowledge of the products she or he sells, and ability to understand the prospect's challenges are essential characteristics to engage potential buyers to take the next step toward the purchase of the product. Therefore, the product manager must ensure that the inside sales organization has the proper training on the product. The product manager should also assist the inside sales representatives in the creation of a script or sales strategy on how they will introduce the product to the prospect. In particular, the product manager needs to educate inside sales representatives on how the product creates competitive advantages for prospects and how they can articulate it to them as quickly as possible during the call. The product manager should also inquire about the questions the inside sales representative is using to understand the prospect's challenges, since more than likely it is what led he or she to make the inquiry about the product in the first place. Understanding the challenges will validate the need for the product or other products the company offers. Furthermore, it will help the inside sales representative make the business case for why the prospect should take the next step toward the purchase of the product. Hence, failure in proper questioning and articulation of the competitive advantages the product creates will adversely affect the prospect's total experience with the company; moreover, it will diminish the value of the product making the prospect more reluctant to pay a premium price.

Legal — Contract Management

The legal department will interface with buyers for negotiating the sales contract. Their role is to act as the liaison between the company and the buyer. Contract managers are utilized to reconcile any variations to both standard and nonstandard contracts and make recommendations. From a sales perspective, they will be involved in sales agreements, distribution agreements, licensing agreements, service level agreements, sub-contracts, master agreements, and non-disclosure agreements.

One of the most critical functions for contract managers is to minimize risk, especially on extremely large deals. Accordingly, contract managers must demonstrate professionalism, a friendly personality, strong skills in sales negotiation, and knowledge of all the contract details. This includes knowledge of the pricing utilizing support from product management; knowledge of financial considerations such as payment conditions, incentives, and rebates utilizing support from finance, accounting, product management, and sales; and knowledge of financial risks such as revenue recognition, pricing and discounting policies, and export regulations utilizing support from finance, accounting, and product management. Any disappointment experienced by the prospect or customer in her or his interaction with the contract manager will diminish the value of the product and the buyer's total experience with the company, making him or her more reluctant to pay a premium price. This also applies to the appearance and the attentiveness of the contract manager to the buyer.

Typically, the product manager will act as an advisor to the contract manager when the need arises to reconcile any variations to both standard and nonstandard contracts. The product manager must take requests for variations seriously; else, it will diminish the value of the product. When the product manager makes an exception to a rule such as a discount policy, it opens the door for more exceptions that eventually will nullify the rule. The best approach is to start by offering the buyer something she or he can benefit from, like a free training class or three months of advance support, instead of circumventing a discount level since the product manager should want to maintain fairness in transactions.

Michael Porter on Buyer Value and the Real Buyer[19]

A firm or household does not purchase a product; individual decision makers do. Both actual value and signals of value are assessed and interpreted by these decision makers. The identity of the specific person or persons who make the purchase decision will influence, if not determine, the value attached to a product. The decision maker may not necessarily be the person who pays for the product (e.g., the doctor, not the patient, chooses drugs) and may be different from the user (e.g., the purchasing agent chooses a product used in the plant). The channel may also make its own decision about whether to stock a firm's product and whether the firm is a desirable supplier.

Different decision makers will value different things about a supplier and use different signals to assess them. A purchasing agent may not value reliability as highly as a plant manager, for example, because the purchasing agent is more detached from the consequences of product failure. The purchasing agent may be motivated more to keep the cost of purchase to a minimum. There may also be more than one decision maker for a product. Both husband and wife typically decide on buying a house, for example, and travel agents and tour brokers all can play a role in choosing an airline or resort hotel. Similarly, the purchasing department and plant engineer often jointly choose pieces of product equipment. A number of individuals frequently influence the decision maker though they may not participate in the decision directly. Such individuals may be able to veto a supplier, despite the fact that they do not have the power to choose.

Identifying the value a firm creates for the buyer and the signals of value used by the buyer, then rest on determining the identity of the real buyer. The process of identifying the real buyer often suggests new dimensions of performance that are not immediately apparent if the buyer is viewed as the firm or household. These can include such factors as prestige, personal relationships with supplier personnel that are valued in their own right, and the desire to avoid personal risk in the purchase decision by choosing a well-known supplier. IBM has exploited its position as a "safe" choice as a supplier, for example, as has Kodak in amateur photography. The expertise and sources of information available to the real buyer will also shape what signals of value will be convincing—an engineer might use technical publications and advertising in technical journals as signals while an accounting clerk might be more swayed by polished salespeople and glossy brochures.

Customer Support and Service

Customer support in the high-tech industry is a range of services available to assist buyers throughout the purchase of a product, from pre-sales to post-sales. The role of customer support is to respond to inquiries and resolve product issues. Typically, customer support provides assistance in the planning, installation, training, troubleshooting, maintenance, upgrading, and disposal of a product.

Most companies offer customer support for its products for either a fee or for free. Typically, free support services include all the support information and tools available on the company's website and access to a generalist for product inquiries through chat, phone, or email. Alternatively, fee base support services may include all or some of the following: installation service, on-site support, parts replacement, return to factory, software upgrades, remote monitoring, and technical support access to a specialist over the phone, or online through chat, email, or a website.

Technical Assistance Center

Over the past decade, technical support through the technical assistance center (TAC) has expanded beyond offering telephone assistance to online support that includes chat, email, and website support. Online support can provide buyers with access to downloadable software and support documents, license key activation, communities and forums, tools to assist in troubleshooting and product assessments, and online TAC support where buyers can open a case. To that end, all of these interactions will have a tremendous effect on the buyer's total experience with a company.

Online Support. A support website can significantly reduce a high-tech company's costs by enabling them to provide buyers with on-demand access to information and tools for assistance in addressing challenges they are experiencing with a product. However, because buyers of high-tech products have mission critical data centers and communication networks, the support website must be implemented as a mission critical resource for buyers. Accordingly, the support website must be easy for the buyer to navigate through in finding support information. The downloadable documents must be clear and well written in their instruction and notification. The community forums must be organized so the buyer can navigate through the discussions quickly; moreover, they must be regularly managed to maintain only helpful and useful information. The support tools including license key activation must be operationally functional, easy to use, and provide worthwhile information for the buyer. Most importantly, cases opened online must be responded to in a timely manner. Should any one of these resources fall short in accomplishing the purpose of their function, it will diminish the value of the product making the buyer more reluctant in the future to pay a premium price.

Telephone Assistance. Although online assistance is becoming more common for support, telephone assistance has been the standard practice for responding to general inquiries and providing mission critical support for buyers in the high-tech industry. Typically, generalists are available during normal business hours to respond to general inquiries from buyers while specialists are typically available 24/7 to handle more complex buyer problems with a product. On the other hand, because website support can significantly reduce costs, most high-tech companies will direct buyers with basic or low severity problems to the support website when they call in for telephone assistance. No matter what, the generalists' and specialists' professionalism, knowledge of the product, caring personality, and ability to understand the buyer's problem are the necessary skills to achieve customer satisfaction when engaging with buyers in need of assistance. Moreover, both generalists and specialists must be able to handle stressful situations, complaints, and problems with an extreme amount of poise. In fact, most technical assistance centers will have a process in place to deal with highly charged customers such as handing the call over to a more senior staff member trained to handle challenging buyer situations. In any event, the objective for the generalists and the specialists is to solve the customer's problem or escalate it to the next level of support so it can be resolved in a timely manner. The longer it takes to resolve the buyer's problem, the more it will diminish the value of the product and the buyer's total experience with the company.

As a result, the product manager must ensure that the generalists and specialists assigned to their product have been properly trained. Moreover, because TAC generally will be the buyer's first line for support, the product manager must ensure that proper support processes are in place to enable the TAC organization to resolve the buyer's problem. For example, the product manager should inquire on how TAC handles the information gathering process and documentation of problems. The objective is to confirm that the right approach is in place to reduce resolution time. The product manager must not leave it up to the TAC organization to figure out because not every product is the same. More than likely the product will have unique characteristics that could get overlooked, lengthening the time to resolution. Additionally, the product manager should meet with the generalists and specialists on a regular basis to get feedback on the product and customer problems reported to the TAC organization. Often their feedback will play a pivotal role in the maintenance releases of the product roadmap. Lastly, since one of the specialists more than likely will be a member of the program team, it is an excellent idea for the product manager to request support metrics from the specialist at least on a quarterly basis. For example, number of calls, severity of calls, range of resolution times, range of response times, number of defects versus instruction support calls, and outstanding or unresolved calls.

Knowledge Base. One of the best resources the TAC organization can create is a knowledge base to assist generalists, specialists, and buyers. A knowledge base is a specific database for knowledge management that can be used to locate troubleshooting guides, support solutions, error messages, known issues, how-to-articles, frequently asked questions, and so on. Consequently, it can be instrumental in reducing the time to resolution of a buyer's problem and improve the buyer's total experience with the company. For that reason, if the TAC organization does not maintain a knowledge base, the product manager should do everything to encourage them to create one. Untimely resolution of the buyer's problem will negatively affect the buyer's total experience with the company and diminish the value of the product, making the buyer more reluctant in the future to pay a premium price.

Installation Service

On-site support for installation typically is a buyer's first contact with the service and support organization; accordingly, the field engineer must demonstrate professionalism, a friendly personality, knowledge of the product, and familiarity with typical customer premises, e.g., data centers. Timely arrival, attentiveness to the customer, and appearance are also essential to avoid diminishing the customer's total experience with the company. No matter what, given the number of uncontrollable variables that can exist at the customer's site, the field engineer's performance in the installation of the product is never guaranteed to go smoothly. Moreover, the longer it takes the field engineer to install the product the more it will diminish the customer's total experience with the company, even if it is due to unknown problems on the customer's premises. Thus, the installation service will diminish the value of the product, making the customer more reluctant in the future to pay a premium price.

A best practice for field engineers assigned to install a high-tech product is to request a consultation meeting with the customer before the installation. This will give the field engineer a chance to verify the customer's requirements and take an inventory of what is currently on-site at the customer's premises. It will also give him or her the opportunity to identify what additional tools and other items might be required as a backup. If the field engineer is unable to schedule and on-site meeting, at the very least the field engineer should set up a call to speak with the customer before the installation. It also helps to ask the customer if they foresee any problems that could arise. The more knowledge the field engineer has about the customer's environment, the better he or she will be prepared should something go wrong. Most importantly, the greater the chance there will be for the installation to go smoothly.

For that reason, it is crucial that the product manager ensure that the field engineers have receive proper training for an installation. In fact, the product manager should sit through the training with the field engineers, so he or she can see firsthand if the installation runs smoothly. It will also allow the product manager to identify potential problems areas that could occur during an installation since there will always be some unknowns at the customer's premises. Additionally, the product manager should take note of the packaging of the product to determine if there is a better way that would reduce the installation time without incident. The point I am making here is that often the blame is placed on field engineer when the installation takes longer than anticipated, but the real problem is in the packaging of the product. Therefore, product managers should solicit feedback from the field engineers on the problems that occurred during the installation of the product since it will diminish the value of the product and the customer's total experience with the company, even if the errors were cause by unknowns on the customer's premises, e.g. data center.

On-site Support

Similar to installation service, on-site support is a customer facing role. In most cases, when TAC cannot resolve an incident remotely, an on-site field engineer will be dispatched to assist the customer. The professionalism, caring personality, knowledge of the customer's problem gathered by the technical assistance center (TAC), and familiarity with typical customer environments, e.g. data centers, is essential for the on-site field engineer to succeed. Timely arrival, attentiveness to the customer, and appearance are also essential to avoid diminishing the customer's total experience with the company.

The objective of the on-site field engineer is to resolve the customer's problem as quickly as possible. A best practice for high-tech companies is to offer additional on-site support services such as preventative maintenance, escalation management for critical issues, on-site training, and/or a resident engineer to reside on-site on a term basis. It does not guarantee that incidents with the product will not occur, but it does provide the customer with a greater level of confidence that the number of problems will reduce and be resolved more quickly. For example, most network equipment companies offer a preventative maintenance service to augment their technical support offering that provides a periodic review of the infrastructure on the customer's premises to optimize network performance. This may involve configuration analysis, product health checkups, software upgrade recommendations, design change, and so on.

No matter what, the product manager must ensure that the on-site field engineers have been sufficiently trained to address incidents and critical issues for the customer in a timely manner. Similar to installation training, the product manager should attend the training for the on-site field engineers to understand the process they will use to resolve the customer's problems and to identify potential problems areas that could arise. Moreover, during this training the product manager should scrutinize the packaging of the product to determine if there is need for improvement. Of course, there will always be some unknowns at the customer's premise that will prevent a 100% assurance in mitigating problems immediately, but the more the on-site field engineer is prepared on the potential scenarios that could arise, the greater chance she or he will have to address the customer's problems in a timely manner. For this reason, high-tech companies should strongly consider offering preventative-maintenance service since it would allow the field engineer to become more intimate with the customer's premises, e.g. data center. Most preventive maintenance services offer inventory tracking and management, so the on-site field engineer can make recommendations on configuration enhancements, software upgrades plans, feature rollouts, and design change strategies. Despite the consequences, the longer it takes the on-site field engineer to resolve the customer's problem, the more of an undesirable effect it will have on the customer's total experience, even if the problem is due to unknowns on the customer's premises. As a result, the on-site support service will diminish the value of the product making the customer more reluctant in the future to pay a premium price.

Additionally, it is the product manager's responsibility to alert customers of potential problems with their products. Typically, the information is in the release notes or through product alerts or advisories. While no customer wants to hear about the existence of problems with a product they purchased, it will allow them to take the necessary steps to prevent or reduce the chance of being impacted. Most importantly, when a product manager has to issue an alert or advisory on their product, a meeting with the quality team must occur immediately to identify ways to improve the product testing process. The issuance of product alerts or advisories cannot be taken lightly. If alerts or advisories occur too often they will diminish the value of the product, making the customer more reluctant in the future to pay a premium price. To minimize the impact product issues will have on the customer's total experience the product manager must work with the quality team to implement a comprehensive testing process for the product.

Lastly, when a situation arises where a problem severely affects a customer sometimes a call from the CEO or a senior executive to the customer's CEO is worth making to assure the customer that the problem will be resolved. Appropriately, the product manager must maintain communication with the sales organization on the volatility of the situation. Too often product managers wait until the situation is explosive before reaching up for help, which is not the right approach. The product manager must stay ahead of the problem by owning the damage control instead of leaving it up to the sales representative since the product manager has the most knowledge about the current and future status of the product. Thus, it is crucial for the product manager to monitor outstanding problems with their products.

Professional Services

High-tech companies offer professional services to assist their customers in the deployment of the products or solutions they purchased. In most cases, this involves implementing a set of best practices to enable the customer to get the most value out of their products. To design a set of services based on best practices it is imperative for the product manager to work with the professional services organization since their product will have unique characteristics from other products. Common best practices include assessment, design, implementation, management, migration, on-site engineers, and technical account managers.

In any case, there are two levels of interaction for the customer with professional services. The first is the best practices used in the services. They have to be comprehensive and proven; otherwise, they will diminish the value the product and the customer's total experience with the company, making the customer more reluctant in the future to pay a premium price. The second is the professional services employees assigned to work with the customer on-site to perform the services purchased. Similar to other customer facing roles, the professional services engineer and technical account manager must demonstrate professionalism, a caring personality, knowledge of the company's products, and vast knowledge of customer environments, e.g. data centers. Typically, the professional services engineers and technical account managers who work in professional services are experts that have extensive experience in high-tech segments such as telecom equipment, security, customer-relationship management software, desktop computing, and so on. In fact, most began their career as a sales system engineer or field engineer and received a promotion into the professional services role because of the knowledge they gained. Moreover, because they approach the customer's challenges based on set of best practices, there is less of a chance to diminish the customer's total experience. That is if the best practices are sound. No matter what, the responsibility of the product manager is to ensure that their products are incorporated into the best practice framework correctly, even when there is no oversight by the professional services engineer or technical account manager on the customer's premises.

Nonetheless, when hiring a professional services engineer from outside the company, the product manager must ensure that she or he has the proper training on the product. Although considered highly skilled in their trade, the product manager should not throw caution to the wind just because the professional services engineer has experience with a competitor's product or has some experience with their product while employed at another company. It will cost the company less to ensure the professional service engineer has the proper training on the product than the costs of diminishing the value of the product and the customer's total experience with the company.

Training

The customer training provided by a company enables the buyer's employees to operate the products they purchased independently; and so, the training must be well defined and comprehensive to ensure the buyer's employees can perform their duties effectively. The objective is to provide sufficient instruction so that the buyer's employees can master the administration of the product. This objective is crucial in the high-tech industry since high-tech products are implemented in mission critical environments where downtime or outages will be extremely costly for the buyer. For that reason, the administrators of high tech products must have adequate training to minimize the chance of those circumstances occurring. As a result, the product manager must ensure that the customer-training design is professional so that the content is meaningful. The instructors should be experts in knowledge transfer of the course material to leave the buyer's employees confident that they can perform their duties in the administration of the products.

Over the past decade, the method for product training has evolved from the classroom and on-site training to integrated training that includes a combination of all or some of the following: instructor led classroom, online instructor led classroom, self-study, and web-based training. Each method can be tailored to provide the best learning approach for the type of instruction delivered. For example, a buyer's employee can take the lecture portion for the product training online and hands-on training on-site or in the classroom. This enables the buyer's employees to maximize their time. It also allows the buyer to lower the training costs for their employees such as travel expenses and the employee's time away from work.

Similar to other customer-facing roles, the classroom and online instructor must demonstrate professionalism, strong communication skills, an engaging personality, knowledge about customer environments, e.g. data centers, and knowledge of the products he or she provides instruction on to the course attendees. Any disappointment the buyer's employees experience in their interaction with the instructor will diminish the value of the product and the customer's total experience with the company, making them more reluctant in the future to pay a premium price. This also applies to the appearance and the attentiveness of the instructor to the buyer's employees. Nonetheless, even though a product manager has little control over the appearance and attentiveness of the instructor, it is the product manager's responsibility to ensure that the instructor is competent in the transfer of product knowledge and use, since he or she engages with the technical employees of the customer.

Michael Porter on Buyer Purchase Criteria[20]

‟ Applying these fundamentals of buyer value to a particular industry results in the identification of a buyer purchase criteria—specific attributes of a firm that create actual or perceived value for the buyer. Buyer purchase criteria can be divided into two types:

- Use criteria. Purchase criteria that stem from the way in which a supplier affects the actual buyer value through lowering buyer cost or raising buyer performance. Use criteria might include such factors as product quality, product features, delivery time, and applications engineering support.
- Signaling criteria. Purchase criteria that stem from signals of value, or means used by the buyer to infer or judge what a supplier's actual value is. Signaling criteria might include factors such as advertising, the attractiveness of facilities, and reputation.

Use criteria are specific measures of what creates buyer value. Signaling criteria are measures of how buyers perceive the presence of value. While use criteria tend to be more oriented to a supplier's product, outbound logistics and service activities, signaling criteria often stem from marketing activities. Nonetheless, every functional department of a firm (and most every value activity) can affect both.

The price premium a firm can command will be a function of its uniqueness in meeting both use and signaling criteria. Addressing use criteria without also meeting signaling criteria, a common error, will undermine a buyer's perception of a firm's value. Addressing signaling criteria without meeting use criteria will also usually not succeed because buyers will eventually realize that their substantive needs have gone unmet.

The distinctions among use and signaling criteria are often complex, since many of a firm's activities contribute to meeting use criteria as well as serve as signals of value. A polished sales force, for example, may both signal value and be a valuable source of applications knowledge that will lower the buyer's cost. Similarly, brand reputation may be valuable to a buyer because it removes any blame if a supplier does not perform ("How can you blame me for selecting IBM?"). Despite such situations, however, it is vital to separate use and signaling criteria and the firm's activities that contribute to both, since only use criteria represent true sources of buyer value. *Buyers do not pay for signals of value per se.* A firm must understand how well it meets use criteria and the value created in order to determine an appropriate price premium. The value of meeting signaling criteria is measured differently. The value of a signaling criterion is how much it contributes to the buyer perceiving the value created in meeting use criteria.

Use Criteria

Use criteria grow out of links between a firm's value chain and its buyer's value chain, as described earlier. Because these links are numerous, there are often many use criteria that go well beyond characteristics of the physical product. Use criteria can encompass the actual product (e.g., Dr. Pepper's taste difference from Coca-Cola and Pepsi), or the system by which a firm delivers and supports its product, even if the physical product is undifferentiated.

While the distinction between a product and other value activities may only be a matter of degree, it remains an important one since other value activities often provide more dimensions on which to differentiate than the physical product. Other value activities besides those associated with the product can represent an important source of differentiation because many firms tend to be preoccupied with the physical product. Use criteria can also include both the specifications achieved by a firm's product (or other value activities) as well as the consistency with which it meets those specifications (conformance). Conformance may be as important as or more important than specifications, although it too is often overlooked as a differentiating factor.

Use criteria can also include intangibles such as style, prestige, perceived status, and brand connotation (e.g., designer jeans), particularly in consumer goods. Intangible use criteria often stem from purchase motivations that are not economic in the narrow sense. Smirnoff Vodka's ability to achieve a premium price for a product that is essentially a commodity stems largely from the social context, in which much drinking takes place. Buyers want to be seen consuming sophisticated vodka or to serve vodka perceived as such by their guest. While intangible use criteria are usually associated with consumers, they can be equally important with other buyers. Owning a Gulfstream III business jet can lead to considerable prestige for executives with their peers, for example. Intangible use criteria are most important in industrial, commercial, institutional products where the real buyer is an individual with considerable discretion in purchasing.

Finally, use criteria also may encompass the characteristics of distribution channels, or downstream value. Since channels can contribute to differentiation, use criteria must reflect these in areas such as channel-provided service, and credit provided by channels. In addition, channels will have their *own* use criteria that measure sources of value in a firm's dealings with them. For example, channels will often want credit, responsiveness to inquiries, or technical support that the end buyer may not notice at all.

Since the performance of a firm in meeting use criteria may also be affected by how the buyer actually uses a product, part of a firm's challenge is to ensure that its product is actually used in a way that allows it to perform to its capabilities. This can be influenced by product design, packaging, and training. Flow control valves, for example, are often designed so they cannot be over torqued. Factors that improve the chances that a product is used as intended often become use criteria in their own right. They may be potential bases for differentiation since firms often assume that their products are used as intended.

Marketing

The marketing department is responsible for the overall branding of the company; hence, the marketing department interacts with customers and prospects through several communication channels. For example, the marketing department interacts through the company's website, public relations, advertising, trade shows, conferences, promotions, webinars, webcasts, and so on. Let's take a closer look at some of these interactions.

The Company Website

A company's website has become one of the hottest real estate in the market for a company. A website's value is priceless when the marketing department realizes the full value it can provide. It is a central location, where prospects and customers can learn everything about a company: the products, solutions, technology, support and service, partnerships, education, financials, executive leadership, corporate responsibility, events, company background, how to contact, and how to buy. Therefore, it must have an image that is attractive, inviting, and tells a story that will lure viewers in.

The website must contain content that is informative, useful, and well written. The branding must be relatable to the company and the value it creates. The graphics must attract the viewer's attention and enhance the content on the website. The video must engage viewers to spend more time learning about the company and the products. Most importantly, the website must be easy to navigate. For that reason, to avoid confusing viewers the website should be no more than four layers deep. Mistakes in branding, content, graphics, video, or navigation will diminish buyers' total experience with the company, making them more reluctant to pay a premium price.

For example, if the branding for a high-tech company is comical, it might appear unreliable. Outdated content or broken links compromises credibility. Cluttered graphics could distract from the message and if the video streaming is slow, the odds of losing the viewer's interest increases.

I have actually experienced every one of these examples and can honestly say that it did diminish my perception of the company and product. Websites, like real estate, require maintenance to keep their value, so it is crucial for the product manager to review the branding, content, graphics, video, and navigation on the website for their product.

Publicity

Publicity is information communicated freely about a product through the mass media. It can produce revenue by advancing a product's reputation with targeted markets. It can also produce revenue by supporting the marketing of products and services. Public relations campaigns have well-defined intentions. They can create awareness, affect opinions, educate markets, and change behaviors about a company or its products.

The most common communications channels a product manager will use for publicity are press releases, blogs, trade shows, conferences, public speeches, advertising, investor relations, and the company website.

The public relations department develops press releases for the product manager to announce the availability of a new product, a new release of the product, a complimentary product through a partnership, or a significant win with a customer. The public relations department can also assist the product manager in writing blogs to voice an opinion about the technology associated with their product.

The marketing communications department organizes trade shows and conferences for the product managers to display their products and meet with customers and prospects. To gain even greater publicity, product managers will present at a conference or trade show. The marketing communications department is also responsible for advertising the product manager's products through advertisements in industry publications online and in print; they also play an instrumental role in the creation of webinars and webcasts.

Despite the consequences, any mistakes that occur in press releases, blogs, or advertising; at trade shows, conferences or during public speeches; with investor relations; or on the company website will diminish the buyers' total experience with the company, making them more reluctant to pay a premium price. For example, misspellings in press releases and blogs; unsuitable attire, poor hygiene, or inattentiveness to customers or prospects at a trade show; or losing the communication feed for a webinar or webcast that causes the product manager to lose half the audience.

Product managers need to be strategic in their use of publicity. The best approach is to have the marketing department create an annual marketing communications plan for the product. The plan should include all the communication vehicles the product manager intends to use such as press releases, product literature, trade shows, and so on. It should also include the budgeted amount for each publicity event. Then, the product manager should meet regularly with the marketing department to ensure all publicity events are on track. The more organized each event is the greater chance for a better outcome.

Executive Leadership

Executive leadership interacts with buyers in several ways, both customer facing and through communication channels. The most common customer-facing interaction is at the customer-briefing center where an executive will stop by to meet with buyers. Then again, on occasion most executives will travel to meet with buyers at their location. Executive leadership is also visible to buyers through video on websites, at conferences where he or she is a keynote speaker, and through television and publication interviews. Additionally, since executives are thought leaders, some will write blogs on the company's website to voice their opinions on the state of the industry. Moreover, buyers can also learn more about executive leadership on the company website where their bios are available.

An executive leader must demonstrate professionalism, a charismatic personality, excellent communication skills, knowledge of the products their company sells, the competitive advantages their products and company creates for buyers, knowledge of their industry, and knowledge of their customers' challenges. Any buyer disappointment when interacting with an executive will diminish the buyer's total experience with the company, making she or he more reluctant to pay a premium price.

Additionally, this applies to the appearance and attentiveness of executive leadership to the buyer. Nonetheless, even though a product manager has little control over the appearance and attentiveness of executive leadership, the product manager must ensure that executive leadership understands the competitive advantages their product creates for buyers. While the product manager may not meet face to face with executive leadership, he or she can accomplish this through their chain of command.

Another way that the CEO will interact with buyers is on the earning call. While the communication mainly addresses shareholders and the financial community, the executive leadership of the company's buyers will also have an interest in the financial health of the company. For this reason, it is essential for the product manager to provide the best commentary on the performance of their product for the current quarter and for the current year. For example, revenue growth (year over year, quarter over quarter, and sequentially quarter over quarter), number of shipments, number of new customers, and significant wins if the buyer agrees to be included in the announcement. Unfortunately, when the product performs poorly in a quarter, it will be difficult, if not impossible, for the company to hide the result, depending on the breadth of products the company sells. As a result, it will diminish the value of the product and buyers' total experience with the company, making them more reluctant to pay a premium price.

Michael Porter on Signaling Criteria[21]

Signaling criteria reflect the signals of value that influence the buyer's perception of the firm's ability to meet its use criteria. Activities a firm performs, as well as other attributes, can be signaling criteria. Signaling criteria may help a particular supplier to be considered and/or may play an important role in the buyer's final purchase decision. Typical signaling criteria include:

- reputation or image
- cumulative advertising

- weight or outward appearance of the product
- packaging and labels
- appearance and size of facilities
- time in business
- install base
- customer list
- market share
- price (where price connotes quality)
- parent company identity (size, financial stability, etc.)
- visibility to top management of the buying firm

Often signaling criteria can be quite subtle. For example, the paint job on a medical instrument may have an important impact on the buyer's perception of its quality even though the paint job has little or no impact on the instrument's performance. Similarly, Arm & Hammer's brand extension into detergents has been perceived as differentiated in part because a box of it is heavier than competitors' products even though it yields the same number of washes.

Signaling criteria are the most important when buyers have a difficult time measuring a firm's performance, they purchase the product infrequently, or the product is produced to buyer specifications and hence past history with other buyers is an incomplete indication of the future. In professional services, for example, signaling criteria are extremely important. Services are typically customized and actually performed only after the buyer has purchased them. As a result, successful professional service firms pay very close attention to such things as office décor and the appearance of employees. Another industry where signaling criteria are important is pianos, where many buyers are not sophisticated or secure enough to judge quality very accurately. Steinway, the differentiated producer, has recognized the use of pianos by concert pianists as a powerful signaling criterion. Steinway maintains a "piano bank" of grand pianos all over the United States that approved artists can use for concerts at a nominal cost. As a result, Steinway has developed excellent artist relationships, and a large percentage of concerts are performed on Steinway pianos.

Signaling criteria also grow out of the need to reinforce the buyer's perception of a firm even *after* the purchase of the product. Buyers often need continued reassurance that they made a good decision in choosing the firm and the product. They may also need education to help them evaluate the extent to which a product is meeting their use criteria. This is because buyers often remain unable to discern how well a product has met their use criteria even after purchase, and may have insufficient data or may not pay enough attention to notice product performance. Regular communication that describes a firm's contribution for its buyers can often have a major impact on differentiation.

Some signaling criteria are associated with particular use criteria, while others are more generalized signals that a supplier will provide value to the buyer. Advertising may emphasize product characteristics, for example, while a firm's reputation may imply to some buyers that many of their criteria will be satisfied. It is important to attempt to draw the connections between signals of value and the particular use criteria they are signaling. This will both help in identifying additional signals of value, and help the firm understand exactly those attributes it's signaling should convey. If a firm recognizes that its customer list is a signal of service reliability, for example, it can present the list in a form that emphasizes this.

In summary, "price is in the eye of the customer" is not as cliché as the fact that most people do not understand what it means. Price is in the eye of the customer means the total experience a buyer has with a company weighed against the price of the purchase the buyer made or makes over a period of time. Total experience means every interaction the buyer has with a company. From the sales process to ordering, delivery, installation, product use, customer support, billing, trade show experience, and so on. Even a company's stock performance is part of the total experience the buyer weighs against the price of the purchase.

While it would be difficult to achieve perfection across all interactions with a buyer, the creation of best practices for interacting with buyers can curb the number of unfortunate experiences a buyer may encounter. Customer-facing roles must demonstrate professionalism; friendly, caring, and inviting personalities; excellent communication skills; knowledge of the buyer's challenges; knowledge of the products they sell; and the competitive advantages the product creates for its buyers. Timely arrival, attentiveness to the buyer, and appearance are also essential.

The sales organization must have access to clear and well-written product literature such as data sheets, white papers, and application notes. They also require access to sales tools such as slide presentations, webinars, video presentations, and webcasts that must be professional in their presentation. Most importantly, they must have access to pricing strategies which convey the competitive advantages that the product creates for its buyers; and also have attractive packaging strategies that streamline the sales order process when buyers purchase products from them.

Customer support and service provide assistance in the planning, installation, training, troubleshooting, maintenance, upgrading, and disposal of a product. Despite the consequences, the longer it takes to resolve a buyer's problem, the more it will diminish the buyer's total experience even if the problem is due to unknowns on the buyer's premises. Preventative maintenance and professional services can help mitigate problem resolution. Most importantly, training must ensure the buyer's employees can perform their duties in the administration of the products.

The marketing department is responsible for the overall branding of the company. Hence, the company website must contain content that is informative, useful, and well written. Most importantly, it must be easy to navigate. The most common communications channels the marketing department will use to assist the product manager in interacting with buyers are press releases, blogs, trade shows, conferences, public speeches, advertising, investor relations, and the company website. Every one of these communication channels has to be executed professionally to create the best, total experience for buyers interacting with the company.

Executive leadership is visible to buyers through video on websites, at conferences where they are a keynote speaker, through television and publication interviews, and through blogs on the company's website. They also engage with customers at their locations and in the customer-briefing center. Their interactions with buyers play a pivotal role in establishing value for the company and its products. Since the executive leadership of buyers will have an interest in the financial health of a company they conduct business with or plan to conduct business with, it is crucial for executive leadership to convey the best performance of the company on the earnings call.

Overall, the critical role of the product manager is to ensure that all customer-facing roles can articulate how their product creates competitive advantages for buyers.

Winning at pricing takes a village. It takes every employee in the company to win since every interaction with a buyer can affect the customer's total experience with the company. For every reader who thought the price of a product was only attached to the product, I hope he or she now understands that price is in the eye of the customer; and so, every interaction can affect price. While flawless would be impossible to achieve, it is still essential that every employee understand the significance these interactions can have on the buyer. Although an employee does not interact with the buyer directly, more than likely she or he is in a role that provides support for someone else who does. Thus, if an employee in a supportive role is underperforming, she or he will indirectly affect the buyer's total experience with the company, making the buyer more reluctant to pay a premium price. For this reason, excellent support for customer-facing roles is instrumental to the success of the product and the company. I wish you "good selling" by winning at pricing!

Index

A
Apple
    effectively signaling value, 15, 16
    positioning the iPhone, 17, 56

B
BOM
    product and gross margin analysis, 22, 23
    packaging analysis, 31–33
    SKU madness, 89, 90
bundling
    downside example discounting the total price, 97
    downside example I/O card, 96
bundling and product line extension Microsoft Office
    example, 92
business case for changing the pricing strategy, 37–40

C
CAPEX and OPEX savings
    service provider edge-router, 26, 62
    solid-state drive (SSD) storage arrays, 57, 58, 81
changing a pricing strategy
    notifying other departments, 51, 52
    politics, 54
    sign off from every department, 53
Cisco
    awards, 73
    collaboration tools, 59
    positioning switches, 17
    premium price, 16, 56
clarity in software licensing
    software licensing strategies, 103
    storage management software example, 101–103
COGS, 22, 23, 31
conducting the packaging analysis, 30–34
conducting the product and gross margin analysis, 22–25
conducting the real world cost of ownership
    analysis, 25, 26

L
lowering buyer cost, 12, 17, 27, 59, 158

M
making value obvious for me too products awards, 73
    certifications, 75, 76
    complementary products or solutions, 72, 73
    finance and leasing options, 71, 72
    strong partnerships, 73–75
    superior customer support and service, 69, 70
    superior professional services, 70, 71
market development funds, 43, 44
marketing
    company website, 161, 162
    publicity, 162–164
Microsoft
    collaboration tools, 59
    Microsoft Office, 92, 97
    Microsoft Office pricing analysis example, 97–99

O
opposite pricing strategy example, 41
outside sales representative
    empowering the sales organization, 138–140
    packaging, pricing, and discounting, 140, 141
outside sales system engineers
    product expertise, 143, 144

P
packaging
    attractiveness of the packaging strategy, 91–101
    clarity of the packaging strategy, 101–104
    complexity of the packaging strategy, 87–91
    customer sensitivity, 86, 87
packaging analysis model, 30, 31
Porter, Michael, 12
    bundled versus unbundled strategies, 100
    on buyer perception of value, 82
    on buyer purchase criteria, 158
    on buyer value, 17
    on buyer value and the real buyer, 146

End Notes and Citations

[1] Michael E. Porter, Competitive Advantage Creating and Sustaining Superior Performance (New York: The Free Press, 1985), 131

[2] Porter 139, 140

[3] Porter 131, 132

[4] Porter 135–138

[5] Porter 115–118

[6] Porter 50–52

[7] Porter 418–422

[8] Source: IBM Power Systems Solid-State Drives (ARMONK, N.Y, IBM, 2010)

[9] Porter 146–150

[10] Porter 127–130

[11] Porter 138–140

[12] Porter 426–429

[13] The Microsoft Office pricing used in this example is Microsoft's published prices on their website at the time this book was written in April 2013 and is subject to change.

[14] Porter 430–432

[15] Porter 237–247

[16] Porter 436–439

[17] Porter 132–135

[18] Porter 135

[19] Porter 140, 141

[20] Porter 141–144

[21] Porter 144–146